SHOOTING FOR SPORT

A GUIDE TO DRIVEN GAME SHOOTING, WILDFOWLING AND THE DIY SHOOT

SHOOTING FOR SPORT

A GUIDE TO DRIVEN GAME SHOOTING, WILDFOWLING AND THE DIY SHOOT

TONY JACKSON

THE CROWOOD PRESS

First published in 2015 by
The Crowood Press Ltd
Ramsbury, Marlborough
Wiltshire SN8 2HR

www.crowood.com

British Library Cataloguing-in-Publication Data
A catalogue record for this book is available from the British Library.

ISBN 978 1 84797 933 9

Typeset by Manila Typesetting Company

Printed and bound in India by Replika Press Pvt Ltd

Contents

Introduction

The basic principle of the shotgun has remained unaltered since the very first 'handgonne' was held, doubtless with some trepidation, by a fourteenth-century soldier who, from the primitive character of the weapon in use, tended to expose himself to rather more danger than the enemy he somewhat optimistically hoped to slay. In those early days hand cannon, in various guises, were largely employed as weapons of war to fire a ball or bullets, and as one might anticipate, these weapons were highly inaccurate. They were, however, calculated to cause dismay amongst an enemy still armed with longbows and crossbows. It was not until the invention of the wheel-lock that guns were used for sporting purposes, and then it was largely on the Continent, for whilst firearms were being used for sport in the fifteenth century in Germany, Spain, Italy, and to some extent in France, it was not until the latter part of the seventeenth century that firearms were employed in Britain for the chase, and then they were mostly of foreign manufacture.

The development of the sporting firearm over the centuries has been related many times. Nevertheless, despite the many variations on a theme, the principle remained the same, namely a projectile to be fired at the quarry, though it was not until the use of 'hayle' shot, or lead pellets, that sporting shooting as we know it today really took off. Two hundred or so pellets, though they might be driven by slow-burning, coarse black powder along the length of a crudely drawn and finished barrel, could still perform remarkable execution when fired at duck, geese or other birds resting on the ground or water or feeding in flocks.

In those early days it was soon appreciated that whilst barrels could be made to ever finer, carefully regulated specifications, igniting the charge was the main problem. The sportsman wandering about with a matchlock, consisting of a loaded gun to be ignited and discharged by a slow-burning fuse, was at a distinct disadvantage as it would have been virtually impossible to stalk deer or other quarry with a glowing match, not to mention the time lag involved in actual ignition. It was not until the invention of rifling in the fifteenth century at Nuremburg, in conjunction with the wheel-lock, that sporting shooting really took off.

The principle of the wheel-lock was simple. A spring revolved against a flint to produce a shower of sparks which ignited fine black powder in a pan, and this in turn activated the main charge in the breech. This early sixteenth-century principle, now established, was refined into the flintlock system: this simply involved a shaped flint held in hammer jaws which, when released against spring pressure by the trigger, struck a steel plate to create a shower of sparks.

The principle remained in use through the seventeenth and eighteenth centuries, and it was only the experiments of an obscure Scottish minister, the Rev. Alexander John Forsyth that resulted in the practical application of the percussion muzzle-loading gun in 1805. The Forsyth lock system involved the use of fulminate of mercury as a detonating agent, and the advantages were at once apparent: it was faster in use than the flintlock system, and eliminated the requirement for fine powder in the pan. From this modest beginning was to develop the percussion cap, which was employed by the muzzle-loader until the invention by the French of the breech-loading system in 1851: this system completely transformed the use of firearms in all their guises.

The development of the shotgun in the nineteenth century was to result in a series of dramatic changes in the shooting field. In the eighteenth century, game, notably partridges, was 'walked up', because the concept of the driven shoot, or *'battue'*, had not yet crossed the Channel. Pheasants were still relatively scarce, and only the grey partridge, and in parts of East Anglia the French or red-legged partridge, were relatively common. The sportsman, armed with a muzzle-loading flintlock and draped with powder and shot flasks, with a servant to carry the bag and accompanied by a brace of pointers or spaniels, would spend his days walking the long-stemmed stubble fields in search of coveys. There was a leisured calm about the day as the sportsman, perhaps with one or two like-minded companions, wandered the peaceful countryside, pausing between each shot, as blue-grey smoke rolled away, to reload his long-barrelled flintlock. Not every shot was guaranteed, for there might be the occasional misfire due to a 'flash in the pan'.

Drastic change is always painful, and even the redoubtable Colonel Peter Hawker, the 'father of wildfowling', was initially reluctant to acknowledge that the percussion or detonating system had made the flintlock redundant. Eventually, however, he was forced to concede that 'for neat shooting in the field, or covert, and also for killing single shots at wild-fowl rapidly flying, and particularly at night . . . its trifle inferiority to the flint is tenfold repaid by the wonderful accuracy it gives in so readily obeying the eye'.

That the pheasant was still relatively scarce on the ground is shown by the fact that Hawker's bag in a season might be no more than half-a-dozen birds, and that he would muster a small army of men to scour the countryside on hearing the report of a vagrant wandering pheasant. On the Continent, however, vast bags of game, small and large, had long been the fashion since the seventeenth century. In 1753, for instance, during the space of twenty days shooting in Bohemia, some twenty-three Guns killed a total of 47,317 head of game, consisting of 19,545 partridges, 18,273 hares and 9,499 pheasants. One might have supposed that by the end of this three-week slaughter the participants would have been sickened, deafened and bored beyond measure.

The Driven Shoot

The *battue*, or driven shoot, when it did arrive on these shores in the early nineteenth century, was by no means received with open arms. An older generation of sportsmen regarded this form of sport as both degenerate and symptomatic of an effeminate age when men could no longer pursue game on foot, but instead stood to have it driven towards them. R. S. Surtees, writing in the 1850s, is bitter in his satire when, writing in *Plain or Ringlets*, he condemns the *battue* as not being 'the thing for able-bodied men; and the fact of their being of foreign extraction does not commend them to our notice'. Nevertheless, whether it was approved of or not, driven shooting was here to stay, and with the invention of the breech-loader, the new mode of shooting quickly became established: now the sportsman could swiftly reload, initially using pin-fire cartridges until these were replaced by central-fire cartridges

Gun Development

However, the transition from muzzle-loaders to breech-loaders did not happen overnight! Many sportsmen who had been brought up with flintlocks and who had eventually accepted the percussion system, were not prepared to forego a lifetime's experience for what they considered might well prove to be yet another gimcrack gunmaker's notion – and for a brief period their suspicions appeared to be justified. The early pin-fire shotguns suffered from several defects, notably an escape of gas from the weak breech closure, whilst the cartridges themselves, with their protruding pins, proved to be singularly dangerous when being carried or handled. The arguments raged back and forth, culminating in breech-loader versus muzzle-loader trials, held by *The Field* magazine in 1858 at Ashburnham Park, Chelsea. The results proved the superiority of the muzzle-loaders, which was not surprising considering the rudimentary condition of those embryonic early breech-loaders, apart from the slowness in loading and the fouling of barrels.

The initial developments of the hammerless breech-loader, the game gun *par excellence* be it side-by-side or over-and-under, were subject to constant experiment and controversy. Not all users of hammer guns were convinced by the appearance of the first hammerless guns in the 1880s, and one well known shot likened the hammerless gun to a spaniel without ears! Sir Ralph Payne-Gallwey, in his book *Letters to Young Shooters*, noted that even in 1890 the two best shots in England, Earl de Grey and Lord Walsingham, were still using hammer guns. However, the merits of the hammerless system were soon evident, and enhanced by steel as opposed to damascus barrels, the ejector system and smokeless powder, the hammerless ejector side-by-side was to dominate the game-shooting scene into the latter years of the twentieth century, and is still regarded as the game-shooting gun *par excellence*.

That Golden Age of driven shooting was indeed brief, and its like will never be seen again – which is perhaps a good thing! Two world wars, and the resultant social and economic upheavals which followed, spelled the end, or restructuring, of many of the large private shoots. Estates changed hands or were broken up piecemeal to pay death duties, game coverts degenerated into bramble-choked wildernesses or were felled, and once bustling keepers' cottages, now deserted, crumbled into ruin. A few private shoots survived on a small scale, but the scene was set for a dramatic change of direction.

The development of the hammerless breech-loader was subject to constant experiment.

The Syndicate Shoot

At the end of World War II, as the country slowly recovered from five years of conflict, those who had fought and survived looked to some form of normality, some reminder of the brief years of peace between the two dreadful wars – and it was now that the syndicate shoot began to emerge. Wealth was more widely distributed, allowing men who in a former life would never have been a part of the private shooting scene, to purchase their way into the sport and social life of the countryside. Syndicates of Guns, in a position to rent shooting at various levels countrywide, began to dominate the shooting scene. Keepers were re-engaged, and a new type of sportsman, perhaps lacking the background or rigorous training, which formerly was considered an essential part of every shooting man's background, began to dominate the scene – and with him them came a welcome breath of fresh air to blow away the musty cobwebs of the past.

Within a few years the syndicate became the mainstay of formal driven game shooting, and for an annual subscription a member was able to buy eight or nine days shooting in a season, the cost varying according to the number of pheasants or partridges released, the status of the keeping staff – whether

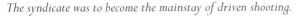

The syndicate was to become the mainstay of driven shooting.

a single keeper or a headkeeper with beat keepers – and the number of birds anticipated to be shot in a day's sport. There was an enormous variation in the composition of syndicates countrywide, a variation that inevitably encompassed an extensive variation in subscription fees.

The 1980s and 1990s saw a new phenomenon: the development of the commercial shoot catering for a class of new would-be shooters, many freshly moneyed from commercial and banking outlets and only too eager to take advantage of their newly acquired wealth. It was not a happy period however, and reports of ignorant, even dangerous behaviour in the shooting field became all too common, resulting in the framing of sporting guidelines for shoots, issued by the organizations defending and promoting the sport. Nevertheless, the commercial shoot was soon to become a respected and viable part of the shooting scene, offering a range of sport to meet most requirements, and today these shoots are an integral part of the shooting scene. The majority tend to offer driven days of around 150 to 250 birds, though a small number can provide much higher bags. In addition, a number of syndicate and private shoots are also prepared to sell several days shooting to assist with running costs.

The wide variety of shooting available has also led to the introduction of the roving syndicate, a group of Guns who prefer variety in their sport as opposed to the predictability of the established shoot. They can, of course, choose and budget for the number of days they can afford, in terms of time and money, while enjoying fresh parts of the countryside and novel sporting situations.

DIY Shoot

The syndicate shoot, in conjunction with both commercial and private shoots, formed the background to the game-shooting scene until recently, when, driven by economic considerations, a fresh approach to the sport appeared in the guise of the DIY shoot. The concept is simple: a group of sportsmen combine to rent either an existing shoot or completely new ground, with a view to undertaking all the rearing and keepering duties themselves; then in the shooting season they operate on an alternate stand and drive basis. No beaters are employed, though family friends are often co-opted to assist on a shooting day. Work parties to build release pens, clear rides and undertake all the tasks of a full-time keeper are required, and this can sometimes prove the shoot's Achilles heel, for too often the workload devolves on to the shoulders of a small but willing group who undertake all the work.

The DIY shoot is expanding countrywide.

This type of DIY shoot is rapidly expanding countrywide, and if one or two members living close to the shoot are willing, and have the time, to take on keepering duties, including feeding, it can prove very successful. Often the shoot will comprise around twenty members, each paying a reasonable subscription to cover the cost of rent, birds and feed, while the farmer on whose land the shoot is operating may himself take a Gun at no cost in return for preparing and sowing game strips.

This type of shoot is flexible, varying from perhaps no more than 200 acres up to a thousand or so, while daily bags may diverge from twenty or so birds to over a hundred. Much depends on the available land, the financial input and how many Guns are involved – but whatever its size and substance, the DIY shoot is expanding, and provides a range of folk with the opportunity to be involved in the sport, folk who might hitherto have baulked at the expense of the syndicate or commercial shoot.

With every DIY shoot, if driven birds are on the agenda, there is an initial cost for the installation of a release pen, or even pens, and then for its continuing maintainance. The next major shoot cost is then the purchase of poults, unless the shoot has the facilities to hatch their own eggs and all that is involved in terms of equipment and feed. If poults are bought in, then growing pellets will be required until the birds are weaned on to wheat.

A major outlay borne by the syndicate and commercial shoot is on beaters and pickers-up, but in the case of the DIY shoot the usual practice is to beat one, stand one: in other words the team of, say, sixteen Guns divides into eight Guns standing and eight beating for the morning, then they swop round for the afternoon. The Guns will only enjoy half the day's sport, but will save the considerable outlay of having to employ a paid beating team. In addition, work parties will be held throughout the spring and summer.

The Rough Shoot

In many ways the DIY shoot has replaced the rough shoot which, half-a-century ago, was the alternative to formal driven shooting. Today the rough shoot, offering modest but mixed bags for two or three Guns, has become increasingly difficult to find as more and more ground has been turned over to driven game shooting in one guise or another. Good old-fashioned rough shooting, offering a wide variety in the bag, can still be found in parts of Wales and Scotland, and occasional corners of England, but it is becoming increasingly uncommon, even though much sought after. I rented one such shoot in West Sussex many years ago, holding 300 acres of rough ground, thick hedgerows, a marsh, dykes and a flight pond. One never knew what might turn up, but a typical bag might have comprised two or three snipe, a woodcock, a hare, the odd pigeon or partridge and perhaps a handful of mallard, wigeon and teal. This was sport of an outstanding nature and today seldom found on that sort of scale.

Inland duck shooting can offer superb sport or prove embarrassingly dreadful. Reared duck have, sadly, acquired a reputation, by no means always justified, of flying low while circling the Guns, or in some extreme cases, refusing even to lift from the water. However, where they are managed correctly they can provide outstanding sport and are well worth considering. Best of all, though, are wild duck attracted to fed-in flight ponds or decoyed on flooded meadows.

For a select band of shooters the finest sport of all is to be found below the sea wall. Today wildfowling, once the pursuit of lone individuals, is now highly organized, with numerous clubs throughout the country affiliated to the British Association of Shooting & Conservation (BASC), the association that started life in 1908 as the Wildfowlers' Association of Great Britain and Ireland (WAGBI).

But just as wildfowling attracts the solitary shooter who prefers his own company on empty shores and mudflats in places little known to many, so too does the pigeon shooter choose to pursue a sport which, in the eyes of many, offers incomparable sport. Woodpigeon shooting, mainly over decoys, has long been a sport in its own right, and although a change in farming practices, including the expansion of rape, has resulted in advanced expertise and methods to outwit the birds, including the use of pigeon magnets, substantial bags can still be made. The woodpigeon population continues to expand, despite the inroads made by shooting, and demands a genuine need to protect farmers' crops.

The Finest Field Sport of All

Much has changed in the world of shooting and conservation over the past forty years, so much so, in fact, that the demand for an update has never been more urgent. An ever-increasing influx of newcomers to the sport is helping to ensure its future, but as I know all too well from correspondence and conversations, many newcomers find entry into shooting daunting – and it is undoubtedly a complex world. Any seasoned shooting man will tell you that he is learning on every outing, for shooting is not just about killing birds and ground game, but involves so much more, and with experience comes

Today's pigeon shooter has to be more sophisticated than his predecessor.

an understanding of wildlife in all its forms and how shooting can play a vital role in the management of the countryside.

In this book I hope to be able to explain the various aspects that surround sporting shooting in all its guises, and if you are a newcomer, to explain the background and fundamentals of what is still, despite our crowded island, perhaps the finest field sport of all.

1
Finding Shooting

Few in the shooting world would argue with my claim that the sporting shooting available in Great Britain today is the envy of the world. Our shooting seasons are of reasonable length, bag limits for wildfowling do not exist and are considered unnecessary, and as far as game is concerned, pheasants and red-legged partridges meet all the requirements demanded for driven shooting, while the red grouse, a bird that is totally wild, is more than holding its own. Sadly, several species are in the doldrums, notably blackgame, capercaillie and, of course, the grey partridge, that delightful gamebird which, until the 1950s and early 1960s, was considered by the connoisseur of driven game to provide the finest sport of all.

Migratory and home-bred wildfowl are, on the whole, holding their own; however, whilst woodcock appear to be maintaining their numbers both in home-bred populations and as winter migrants, snipe have shown a slight decline over the past twenty-five years, both in migratory birds and those which are home-based. One bird that is regarded as a pest by farmers and a sporting delight by shooters is the woodpigeon, and this bird has been responsible for establishing a sport in its own right. Decoyed pigeon shooting was really launched as a sport demanding fieldcraft, dedication and a knowledge of the countryside and its seasons by the late and great Major Archie Coats. Not only was Archie a brilliant shot, he was also responsible for developing the use of decoys, hides and all the cunning that is essential if one is to bring home reasonable bags. As a professional pigeon shooter Archie would average around 16,000 birds a year, often killing two or three hundred in a day, and at one time held the record bag of 550 pigeons, shot on 10 January 1962.

In those far-off days, when pigeon decoying, Archie simply wore tweeds and a floppy hat, shooting from a hide cut out of a hedge with a billhook or from a pile of straw bales – a far cry from today's pigeon shooter who feels it essential to be clad from head to toe in camouflage gear and to shoot from an elaborate hide over a magnet decoy . . . but then pigeon are today far more sophisticated and wily than their 1960s ancestors, and there is also far more rape than was the case in the 1960s and 1970s. Rape is a plant much loved by pigeon, and it also provides the grey hordes with ample choice of dining area: this means that the pigeon decoyer can all too often find himself chasing flocks from field to field and to little purpose.

Today, visitors from overseas – notably Americans, French, Germans, Danes and Italians – swarm to this country to sample the wide range of superb shooting we can offer, whether driven or walked-up game, or pigeon shooting over decoys. Driven shooting for pheasants and red-legged partridges, with substantial bags and high, testing birds, is not cheap, but those who buy such a day know that, of its type, it is the best in the world; while at the top of the table, the red grouse offers a unique, if highly expensive shooting experience, whether driven or walked up over dogs.

Options Available Today

Nevertheless, entrance to the sport today, in whatever guise, is far more accessible than it was some forty or fifty years ago. There was, indeed, a period between the world wars when rough shooting could be picked up for a modest fee or even for a bottle or two of whisky at Christmas – but times and attitudes soon changed after World War II when the demand for shooting in the 1950s and 1960s began to outstrip the supply. In those years the classified columns of the weekly *Shooting Times* magazine were filled with requests for rough and pigeon shooting, interspersed with the occasional offer of guns on syndicated shoots. Commercial and DIY shoots were still a thing of the future.

Indeed, for many years the rough shoot provided an outlet for anyone seeking sport at a reasonable cost, while at the same time often offering a wide variety of sport. But how do you define a rough shoot? In broad terms, it is any shooting where game is not reared and which lacks a keeper. The game, winged and ground, is totally wild, and the acreage, while it may be relatively small, can often produce outstanding sport. The late Noel 'Tim' Sedgwick, a former and renowned editor of *Shooting Times*, before the last war paid the princely sum of £2 for the shooting rights over forty-eight acres of water-meadow beside a river, and in one season shot twenty-one brace of partridges, thirty-one pheasants and over 300 snipe, not to mention numerous duck, hares, rabbits and pigeons. That is rough shooting at its very best!

Such sport is as rare as duck's teeth, and anyone who has access to a rough marshland with drains and some cover has a pearl beyond price. Today, rough shooting is still to be found in the more remote parts of Wales and Scotland, but in much of England the rough shoot of the past has now evolved into the DIY game shoot – of which more later. Occasionally, though, one can still discover a small acreage holding a few wild pheasants, some rabbits and, if one is fortunate, a duck-friendly pond that can be cared for, fed and shot in moderation. The rent, however, will be rather more than £2!

Options Available to the Complete Beginner

So what are the options available to the complete beginner, the man or woman who has an urge to enter the shooting field but is uncertain in which direction to set out, or how to go about it? My advice to the novice is always the same: don't even think about buying a gun at this stage, but instead read! Borrow or buy books dealing with the history and background of shooting in this country, soak up the classics, read the works of renowned writers such as Sir Ralph Payne-Gallwey, Noel Sedgwick, 'BB' (Denys Watkins-Pitchford), Colin Willock, Gough Thomas, Fred J. Taylor, John Humphreys, Archie Coats and W. W. Greener, to name but a handful of the leading sportsmen of their time.

Search out, discover and absorb the history and background to shooting in Britain and how it evolved through the nineteenth century, from the days of walked-up sport with muzzle-loading flintlocks in the early part of that century, to the last decade when driven shooting was at its zenith and the side-by-side breech-loading ejector dominated the field. A knowledge and understanding of the background and history of the sport, and how it has adapted in accordance with changing social circumstances, will serve not only to educate the beginner but also to enable him or her to understand something of the crucial role that shooting plays in the management of the countryside and its wildlife.

Armed with some background knowledge of the various branches of shooting available, the beginner has a variety of choices that will depend on personal inclinations, available budget and the influence of any friends or acquaintances who may already be involved in the sport. At this stage it would be wise not even to consider acquiring a gun until you have a reasonably clear concept in your mind in which direction you intend to go. The purchase of a shotgun can be fraught with hazards, as I know only too well, and it is all too easy to find yourself the proud possessor of an over-priced, ill-fitting and totally unsuitable shotgun.

Join the Beating Team

At this early stage contacts are essential! So much, of course, depends on where the beginner lives. If he or she is already established in the countryside, then the doors should readily open to provide a range of opportunities. Without question, one of the most fruitful and rewarding contacts will be a local driven shoot. An offer to join the beating team during the shooting season will seldom be refused, and will usually prove an invaluable source of contacts and advice.

A season's beating, quite apart from providing exercise and a modest monetary reward, will bring into perspective the entire panorama of game shooting, and will invariably draw the sociable and inquisitive beginner along the paths that lead to experience and knowledge. The sport of shooting is not simply a question of handling and firing a gun at living quarry, an approach adopted by all too many so-called shooting men whose notion of sport is gauged by the number of cartridges they have fired in a day. They have little real interest in the countryside, in its moods, its rhythms and its wildlife, all of which are a reflection of the country scene and all it entails.

Take Shooting Lessons

If one is sufficiently well off it is, of course, simple enough to make contact with a well run clay shooting ground, and to take the advice of a professional shooting instructor. The novice will be offered the best possible guidance and be given a series of shooting lessons, during the course of which the instructor will swiftly discover his pupil's ability or otherwise, will iron out any obvious handling faults, and using a try-gun (a gun, the stock of which can be altered to meet the physical demands of its user), will determine exactly the measurements required when purchasing a new gun.

Shooting lessons are not cheap but they are invaluable, and every newcomer to the sport should make it a matter of practice to visit a shooting ground before ever considering buying a gun. The initial outlay in lessons and the expertise of the instructor will be a mere drop in the ocean compared with the money that could be wasted in acquiring an ill-fitting gun and enduring the resultant poor shooting, frustration and acquired bad mounting habits. Time and again I have watched Guns in the driven shooting field who, season after season, spend a small fortune on their sport but appear to derive very little enjoyment as they shoot so badly. It never seems to occur to them to sort out the root cause of the problem at a shooting school, and so they continue, year after year, missing and wounding birds, killing the odd one, but never sure how or why, and deriving little real enjoyment or satisfaction from the day's sport.

The Clay Shooting Club

The novice shot and the complete beginner must acquire some basic knowledge and groundwork before ever considering subscribing to a driven game syndicate or even joining a small and modest DIY shoot. Better by far to join

Shooting lessons are invaluable.

a clay shooting club that offers sporting shooting layouts and the advice of experienced members. Diving straight into the driven game scene, with no background experience, can be a sure recipe for disaster and unnecessary expenditure.

Entry to the Shooting World

Today there are far more opportunities for the novice to enter the shooting world than was the case forty years ago, and one branch of shooting, namely

Wildfowling offers the novice shot a wealth of experience.

wildfowling, still offers the opportunity not only for the beginner to become immersed in what many folk would regard as the finest sport of all, but also to receive instruction from experienced shooting men who, in almost all cases, are only too willing and happy to help someone who wishes to join their ranks.

My own entry into the shooting world provided a perfect example of what not to do! At the age of sixteen I bought a battered old 12-bore hammer-gun for a fiver. Fortunately I never fired the wreck, as an experienced and older friend pointed out that it was almost certainly out of proof, the barrels were damascus, and it was so loose at the joint that it rattled when he held it at the wrist and shook it! The next gun cost a tenner, and whilst it came from an excellent stable and appeared to be tight and in proof, not only was it a hammer-gun, but it also had a severely offset stock, having been built for a right-handed shot with a left master eye. As a result, whenever I fired the gun I had to close my right eye, which was my master eye, in order to hit anything. I used this gun for several years, by which time, when I shifted back to a straight stock, I could not stop closing my right eye, instead of shooting with both eyes open!

Join a Club

All this is by way of pointing out the hazards surrounding ignorance. My real entrance to the world of shooting was via a wildfowling club on the south coast. Chichester Harbour Wildfowlers' Association proved a superb training ground. In those distant days several waders were still on the shooting list, including redshank, curlew and bar-tailed godwit, and though I spent many happy days alone on the foreshore, I soon teamed up with several experienced club members, and through their kindness and advice acquired a reasonable knowledge both of the wildfowling and general shooting scene.

In those distant days the sport of wildfowling was administered by the Wildfowlers' Association of Great Britain & Ireland (WAGBI), the association

---

Safety

The one basic rule, whether you are shooting pigeons on your own, standing at a peg on a driven shoot, or simply clay busting, is total and complete safety!

You are handling a weapon that, in the wrong or careless hands, can be lethal. Anyone who has spent a lifetime in the shooting field will have witnessed dangerous shots, and if unlucky, may have been victim to a shot that should never have been fired. There have been deaths, often accidentally self-inflicted, particularly in the days when hammer-guns were commonplace and foolish Guns dragged them through hedges or rough cover with the hammers cocked, while there have been all too many cases of Guns and beaters receiving an uncalled-for dose of pellets. Eyes have been lost and other serious injuries sustained through carelessness, ignorance and sheer stupidity.

All too often, shotgun accidents have taken place on driven shoots, particularly on grouse moors when over-excited and often novice Guns have swung through the line of butts as a pack of grouse whirled over. A hasty shot and the next door Gun has been hit in the face! Woodcock, too, have all too often been the cause of an accident when, flying low out of cover on a driven day, the sight of this much prized bird has overcome caution and a low shot has struck a fellow Gun or perhaps a beater emerging from the woodland. Such was the reputation of this bird as a prime source of accidents that some Guns and beaters would fling themselves flat on the ground if a woodcock flew from cover!

Every shotgun must at all times be treated as though it were loaded. If a gun is handed to you, perhaps to examine and it is closed, it must be immediately opened and the chambers checked. Similarly in the field, if you are walking up with a loaded gun in anticipation of a shot, the gun must be broken and cartridges removed whenever an obstacle such as a ditch, bank or gate is encountered; and if you have a companion with you, the empty gun must be shown to him for reassurance.

founded in 1908 and which in 1979 was to change direction and title. Despite a degree of unease exhibited by grass-roots wildfowlers, the British Association for Shooting & Conservation (BASC) was born, and today promotes and defends all aspects of live shooting.

However, you may not live near the coast, and whilst wildfowling may figure on your agenda when you are more experienced, you may prefer to pursue a more conventional route into the shooting world. It is, of course, perfectly feasible for a complete novice to buy a day's shooting on a commercial shoot, but it would be foolish to follow this course. Disaster would rule the day!

In my view, the first and most important step, long before you think of buying a gun or even taking shooting lessons, is to join BASC, the association which, as previously noted, administers, supports and defends all aspects of live shooting in Britain and Northern Ireland. Not only will you receive the benefit of massive public liability insurance, but you will have access to advice and information. BASC will not find you shooting, but its experts can offer advice and practical help and point you in the right direction. The association attends numerous country shows throughout the year, and through its shotgun coaching schemes has introduced thousands of beginners to the sport and pointed them in the right direction. In addition, scores of wildfowling clubs and associations are affiliated to BASC, and many provide the opportunity for the complete beginner to take his or her first steps into the world of shooting.

My own club, the Devon Wildfowling and Conservation Association, like many another club, operates an excellent scheme for complete beginners, which entails their being mentored by an experienced club member until both parties are satisfied that the newcomer to the sport has gained sufficient knowledge of the area and the hazards of tides and weather, and is also able to identify quarry and birds that are protected.

In addition, the novice must be aware of public relations. He or she may well be shooting, perfectly legitimately, in an area frequented by the public, and whilst the wildfowler normally operates on his own at dawn and dusk, bird watchers may be encountered and their activities must be respected.

The Personal Approach

In the past, advice along the lines of finding shooting usually adopted the 'knocking on doors' strategy. In other words, the seeker after shooting was advised to approach farmers and landowners to enquire whether there was any pigeon or rabbit shooting on offer. Very occasionally this approach

If you shoot then you should belong to BASC.

might have worked, especially if a farmer was besieged by hordes of raven-
ing woodpigeon, but in the majority of instances the shooting had already
been snapped up by a local who was well known to the farmer, or the game
shooting was already rented to a syndicate who also looked after the pigeon
and rabbit control, or the farmer preferred to keep the sport for himself and
friends. That is not to say that pigeon shooting cannot be found by a direct
approach, or through contacts who know the farmer or land owner, but
today it is seldom a first port of call.

Woodpigeon shooting, itself a superb and testing sport, today still provides
a genuine and vital form of crop protection, but for the novice it can be a surprisingly complicated sport which, if genuine crop protection is to take place,
demands an in-depth knowledge of the birds, how they react to weather
systems, to different crops and in the seasons of the year. Woodies are now
surprisingly sophisticated, and the decoying methods of the past no longer

An approach to a farmer can occasionally result in some pigeon shooting.

achieve fruitful results today. The modern successful decoyer will probably be using a magnet decoy system linked to a sophisticated layout of decoys.

There are, however, several professional woodpigeon shooters country-wide who each operate over thousands of acres to provide a protection service for farmers, and who also supplement their income and extend their shooting coverage by taking paying shooters as guests on their outings. This is an excellent way of obtaining what can often be superb and testing shooting. This is a sport which demands discipline and a degree of experience if reasonable bags are to be made. Once again, the complete novice is advised to consult the experts through reading. One of the best books on the subject, and a classic in its own right, is *The Pigeon Shooter* by John Batley, sub-titled *A Complete Guide to Modern Pigeon Shooting* (Swan Hill Press).

Beating on a Driven Shoot

Today, many beginners enter shooting by way of offering their services as beaters on a driven shoot. This is one of the best ways of learning from the bottom up, and while it requires a degree of dedication, it has several positive benefits. Don't assume that every driven shoot will require new faces, but persistence and keenness will invariably pay off in the long run. If you

An offer to beat on a shoot can often pay dividends.

live in, or reasonably near the countryside, one can usually discover the location of nearby shoots, and having done so, contact with a keeper, or the head-keeper, can often be made through his 'local', or simply by calling on him. You can also make contact with other beaters through your nearest clay shooting club or instruction ground.

As a beater you will quickly discover how a driven shoot operates, make useful contacts and, assuming you are sociable and reasonably outgoing, find yourself becoming embroiled in the local shooting world. Many driven shoots have a day's sport at the end of the season, which is reserved for the beaters, and they also allow roost shooting for pigeons in February and March, and organize vermin drives to assist the keeper. One other advantage of joining the beating line is that you may also be paid for your services! This is not the case with every shoot, for some smaller operations or DIY shoots may instead offer a brace of birds at the end of the day, and when the shooting season is ended, a slap-up meal for the entire team.

As a novice beater you will note that several of your companions work more than half decent gundogs in the line. These are usually springer spaniels, though I have seen a variety of breeds, ranging from terriers to collies, and surprisingly working under reasonable control. The novice is unlikely to have an asset of this nature, but if he chooses to continue as a beater, quite apart from any shooting he may obtain, then a gundog is essential – but more of this later.

In Summary

Summing up, then, the options for the complete beginner who wants to enter the world of shooting are relatively simple. Before he or she even thinks about buying a gun or a place in a shoot, a course of shooting lessons with a thoroughly competent shooting instructor should be the first step. You will quickly discover whether or not the sport is for you, and assuming that you persist, will receive professional advice regarding gun fit, master eye and the type of shotgun you should be looking for. At this point let's move on to the next chapter.

2
Gun Safety

I should make it clear straightaway that I am not an expert in ballistics, and can all too readily appreciate the bewilderment of the novice when faced with the need to make sense of chokes, barrel lengths, bore sizes, patterns, shot loads, raised ventilated ribs, polychokes . . . the list seems endless, the confusion unlimited. All this can be resolved readily enough, but before we do so the beginner must understand one vital, yet simple fact: a shotgun is designed to kill living creatures, and that can include man. At relatively short range this smooth-barrelled weapon can cause devastating damage to the human frame.

I have had the misfortune to see someone killed in the shooting field, shot by a man who had preached safety all his life but who, in the heat of the moment, took a chance. This was, admittedly, during the course of a driven wild boar shoot in what was then Czechoslovakia, and the man involved was using a .308 rifle. His victim was a beater dressed in a long brown coat who had taken a shortcut. I was in charge of the party and will never forget the appalling scene or the near suicidal shooter. Not a shotgun, admittedly, but an example of the consequence of careless misuse of a deadly weapon in the field.

The novice, the beginner to shooting, must understand that at relatively short range a charge of shot can have a gruesome effect, and this is best illustrated by firing at a large cabbage or cauliflower six feet away. The vegetable will be blown to bits, and one can all too readily imagine the effect on soft tissues or the human skull. It is a basic and essential safety tenet to assume that every gun is loaded, and it must never, under any circumstances, be pointed at anyone or in their direction.

In Britain, the shooting world, be it shotgun or rifle, has an excellent reputation for safety, but nevertheless accidents are recorded each year. Driven grouse shooting has produced more than its fair share of accidents, usually caused by a novice shooting at birds crossing low over the butts and failing to remember that another Gun is twenty yards (metres) away and only his face may be showing. The excitement of the sudden appearance of a covey bursting on the scene can all too readily result in a severe accident.

A charge of shot can have a devastating effect at close range.

Beaters, too, can be vulnerable to a low shot fired at a bird as they approach the end of a drive, while a woodcock flying low out of cover and down the line of Guns has traditionally been a hazard and a cause of accidents. Remember, too, that a charge of shot fired at around 45 degrees may carry up to 200 yards, and although the pellets will be widely scattered, a single one could still put out an eye.

Carrying a Gun Safely

In the field, whether in company or alone, there are only two safe ways in which to carry a gun: with the barrels pointing at the sky or the ground. The gun should be carried at the high port or through the crook of the arm with the barrels pointing at the ground. It can be carried on the shoulder but with the trigger guard uppermost. Never have the guard down, as the barrels will then be horizontal and could be pointing directly at any one behind. Never carry the gun at the trail or balanced across one's body, an unpleasant habit which is seen all too frequently. Walking on the left of someone carrying a gun pointing at your stomach can be rather more than alarming, and this potential act of dangerous stupidity should be pointed out, even if offence is taken.

OPPOSITE: *Carrying a shotgun safely … open and pointing at the ground.*

Another habit, which is safe but looks sloppy, is to carry the gun by the barrels, broken and resting on the shoulder. It is perfectly safe, and while frequently adopted by clay shooters, is nevertheless seldom seen in the formal shooting field. Again, if you are walking and expecting a shot, the gun should be carried at high port, the barrels pointing to the sky and the butt resting against your hip.

The safety catch should remain on at all times, only being released as a shot is being taken. Pushed forwards by the thumb as the gun is raised, this will eventually become an automatic reaction, though it will initially require conscious thought to achieve. Never walk or stand with the safety catch off: you could trip or fall with a resultant discharge and possible accident. Always and without exception, break your gun and show that the chambers are empty when you are in company.

There will also be numerous occasions in the field when you have to cross an obstacle such as a fence or wire, or a ditch or gate. Your gun must be unloaded before you attempt to cross over, and if you have a companion, allow him to cross first while you hold both guns, making sure they are empty, then check each gun and hand it across in turn by the barrels. Never at any time lean a gun against a gate, a car or any hard surface: it may appear safe but could easily be knocked over by a passing dog, and if, by hideous chance, you have left it loaded, the safety catch could be jarred off and the gun discharged.

Passing a gun across a gate, broken and empty.

Remember that the safety catch only bolts the triggers so they cannot be pulled, but the gun does not become uncocked: the internal hammers are still poised over the cartridge heads, and are only prevented from being activated by a sear resting in a shallow notch in the hammer. Total reliance on a gun being safe because the safety catch is on can be highly dangerous, and at all times the barrels or barrel must be pointed at the sky or the ground.

Up to around fifty or so years ago it was the practice on formal driven shoots for that older generation always to carry their guns closed between drives, and photographs of shoots taken before the last war will invariably depict all the sportsmen, when standing in formal groups, carrying their guns closed. The reasons offered were specious, and revolved around an unwritten understanding that all one's companions were safe and their guns would invariably be unloaded, whilst it was also claimed that there was a possible danger of rain getting into open locks or strain being placed on open barrels. Today, anyone seen between drives with a closed gun would be politely but forcibly asked to show that it was empty.

Hammer-Guns and Safety

What of hammer-guns and safety? These fine old war-horses are still frequently encountered in the shooting field, and for many years I have used a hammer-gun made by Cogswell & Harrison in 1878. The barrels are damascus, as one would expect, there is scarcely a hint of choke in either barrel, yet it shoots a quite superb pattern. Obviously originally built for black powder cartridges, on the advice of a gunmaker I took the chance and submitted the old gun to nitro-proof several years ago. It sailed through and I have used it ever since with 28g loads of No. 6 or 7. However, I am frequently asked *when* one should cock a hammer-gun in the field.

Should the gun be cocked as it is brought to the shoulder, or should both hammers be ready cocked at all times? If I am standing by a covert side waiting for pheasants to be brought forwards, then I can see no reason why both hammers should not be at the ready. However, if walking up game, then I would normally have the gun uncocked unless I was anticipating an immediate shot. In this case the gun should be held at the high port position with the barrels pointing at the sky. When lowering the hammers it is far safer again to adopt the high port position. If the gun is pointing at the ground when lowering a hammer it is all too easy for your thumb to slip, with a resultant discharge. Cocking a hammer-gun as you raise it to your shoulder is awkward and could lead to a premature discharge, whilst it is impossible to cock both hammers at once.

A bad habit! Gun held across the body, pointing at another Gun.

Never carry a gun at the trail.

Taking a low shot down the line.

A hammergunc in use with barrels pointing skywards.

The basic rule of gun safety in the field, at home, or wherever the weapon is handled, is that it must never, at any time, be pointed at anyone, even though you may know, beyond doubt, that it is unloaded. In addition, your fingers must at all times be kept away from the triggers, only touching them when you are taking a deliberate shot.

Beware 20-Bore Cartridges

In addition to the basic safety rules there is a *caveat* regarding 20-bore cartridges. An appalling risk can be posed, one resulting in terrible injury or worse, if by ill chance one of these cartridges inadvertently finds its way into a cartridge bag holding 12-bore cartridges.

The usual scenario is as follows: a Gun, using a 12-bore and busily employed by the covert side, dips a hand into his cartridge bag, loads and fires, but simply hears a click, and in the heat of the moment assumes a misfire. He opens the gun, sees that there is no cartridge in the chamber, and assumes he forgot to reload. A 12-bore cartridge is chambered, the gun fired – and the barrel is torn apart, almost certainly severely injuring the shooter's forward hand, or worse. He had, inadvertently, loaded a 20-bore cartridge, which had slipped beyond the chamber to rest on the cone at the

Beware mixing yellow 20-bore cartridges with 12-bore cartridges.

entrance to the chamber proper. The 12-bore cartridge explodes the smaller cartridge with a resulting serious burst.

Even though 20-bore cartridges are normally yellow and should be readily identified, if in the heat of action one has found its way into a bag of 12-bore cartridges, there is always a potential hazard lurking. The safest option is not to have 12-bore and 20-bore cartridges in the same house.

Guns can also burst if plugs of mud or snow block the muzzles and are not noticed by the shooter. This is one reason for carrying a collapsible cleaning rod when wildfowling or shooting under conditions that allow for this type of hazard.

'Bargain'-Priced Guns

Another insidious danger can be posed by old 'bargain'-priced guns. There was a time when cheap foreign guns, often of Belgian origin, could be found lurking in farms, sheds or through private sales. All too often these guns, which cost perhaps a fiver new, would be constructed to basic specifications and would reveal excessive head space, cracked stocks or pitted

Modern gunshops have eliminated 'rubbish' guns.

barrels. I have seen, in the past, ancient shotguns with broken wrists held together with rivets or wrapped round with wire, and guns that rattled and shook when held by the stock and shaken. Fortunately, these horrors are rarely seen today, and if found, are confined to being displayed as wall pieces.

Modern proof and a highly organized gun-shop service have today eliminated the rubbish guns that were once all too prevalent.

Pigeon Shooting Over Decoys

Pigeon shooting over decoys can offer a raft of safety issues, especially if there are two Guns in the same hide. Under these circumstances discipline is essential in order to avoid a clash of barrels, an inadvertent discharge, or worse, and there should be an agreement that each Gun shoots in turn, and that both should never be discharged at the same time. Birds coming in to the decoy pattern may often be at head height, and normal safety discipline, demanding sky around the bird, will not apply. It is essential, then, to know the siting of any public footpaths or rights of way. Be aware, too, of bridle-paths and the possible danger arising from a horse being startled by a shot and throwing its rider.

Two Guns in a pigeon hide calls for safety discipline.

If you leave a hide to collect dead birds or to rearrange the decoys, always make sure your gun is unloaded and left on the ground, not propped up against a stake or background hedge. In addition, if you have a dog in the hide, enforce discipline at all times. Do not allow it to run in whenever you shoot, knocking the hide and perhaps pushing you off balance with a loaded gun in your hands.

Safety at All Times

Safety at all times is a matter of common sense. Guns are designed to kill, and if mishandled or treated with the slightest disrespect, an appalling accident involving severe injury or the loss of human life may be the outcome. I repeat, never point a gun, even though you know it is unloaded, at anyone or in their direction. If by ill chance or sheer stupidity you acquire a reputation for being unsafe in the shooting field, you will find all too swiftly that you are shooting on your own.

3
Choosing a Gun

This neatly brings us to the simple question: what is a shotgun? Basically, a shotgun is a smooth-bored weapon, lacking any rifling in the barrel and which is intended to fire cartridges, usually loaded with lead pellets or, where new legislation requires, pellets derived from a non-toxic material such as steel or bismuth. Abroad, if large game such as driven wild boar is on the agenda, a single solid lead ball, armed with vanes to ensure it spins, may be used. At reasonably close range, say ten to fifty yards, this projectile is deadly. I have shot driven wild boar in Tunisia using my ordinary side-by-side game gun armed with Brenneke solid ball cartridges, and found the combination to be highly effective.

Gun Types

The shotgun itself may have only one barrel, or it may have two, set either side-by-side or over-and-under; it is identified by the nominal size of the bore, so that in Britain we have the option of a 4-bore, 8-bore, 10-bore, 12-bore, 16-bore, 20-bore, 28-bore or a .410. The significant numeral, other than in the last case, is an indication that, for instance, in the case of a 12-bore, twelve spherical balls, each exactly fitting the bore, would weigh one pound, and the average diameter of the bore would be .729in. The little .410, however, is the exception to the rule as the figure is the actual calibre size, revealing the internal barrel diameter in decimals of an inch.

Both 4-bores and 8-bores are still used by a handful of dedicated wildfowlers, and specialist cartridges can still be obtained, though they are extremely expensive. The 8-bore can fire a 2oz load which, in theory, can down a goose or duck at sixty yards (metres), while the 4-bore load of 3¼oz is alleged to throw a pattern capable of pulling down a goose at eighty yards. However, such feats can only be achieved through years of experience. The 10-bore also has a modest if enthusiastic following amongst wildfowlers, but it is the 12-bore which, in all its many guises, has been, and still is, the workhorse of the shooting world, even though the 20-bore has long been snapping at its heels in the game-shooting world. On the Continent, the 16-bore has long

Top, an over-and-under, sidelock 12-bore and camouflaged semi-automatic.

12-bore side lock with side-plate removed.

been favoured, though has never proved popular in the UK, where it is occasionally encountered.

Over the past half century the 20-bore, in side-by-side or over-and-under format, has steadily gained an enthusiastic audience. Lighter than a 12-bore, it handles easily and because it is capable of firing a load of 1oz, can compete on virtually level terms with its big brother, the 12-bore. I am not, I confess, a great enthusiast for the 28-bore, which can only handle a ⁹⁄₁₆ oz load in a 2½ in cartridge. I have seen it used on game shoots, and whilst an exceptional shot may be capable of making a showing with this very small bore, in the hands of the average shot it would prove inhumane or frustrating through wounding or missing.

As for the little .410, this can be useful enough shooting rats or very close rabbits, but I have always found its long barrel and rifle-like handling qualities ungainly, and I would never choose to start a beginner on one of these little guns. Thousands of single-barrelled .410 shotguns were imported to this country from the Continent in the early part of the last century. Cheaply made and low priced, with 2in chambers, these old wrecks can still be found today but should be avoided at all costs. Many were made as so-called poachers' guns, with hollowed-out folding stocks. For the youngster who is being entered to shooting their only merit lies, in my view, in their use as a means of teaching safety. Where live quarry is concerned they should be avoided.

Side-by-side .410s are also available and do at least have the merit of being reasonably balanced, unlike the single-barrelled guns in this bore. However, they are usually expensive, and whilst handsome enough, whether hammerless or with hammers, are still not genuine competitors where 12- or 20-bores are concerned.

The remaining gun types are the single-barrelled shotguns, which can be divided into three categories. In the first there are the guns with drop-down barrels, whose actions may be hammerless or with hammers. Cheap single-barrelled guns are usually intended as working tools that can be used for grey squirrel control, or to deal with pests such as magpies, crows or rabbits. They will never, of course, be seen in the game-shooting field.

The second category covers repeaters, which include pump-action guns whose fore-end slides back and forth by hand to eject empty cartridges and reload live ammunition, and bolt-action guns. Lastly, we have the semi-automatics, which are divided into recoil-operated guns, such as the renowned Browning, and gas-operated guns. These types of action, including pump-action, are now limited by law to having a permanently restricted magazine capacity of no more than two cartridges.

The semi-automatics are popular with both wildfowlers and pigeon shooters, but will never be seen in the game-shooting field as they have the considerable disadvantage that they score badly from a safety point of view. A side-by-side or over-and under can, and should, be carried at all times with the barrels broken and the chambers empty when not in use, a condition that can readily be noted by an observer; repeaters and semi-automatics, on the other hand, lack this facility and even when the gun is unloaded, there is no means of knowing whether or not the chamber still holds a cartridge.

Another disadvantage that applies to semi-automatics and repeaters is the danger – particularly on the foreshore – of an obstruction in the barrel, such as mud or snow. With a side-by-side or over-and-under it is a simple matter to break open the barrels and check for any obstruction which, again, can usually be readily cleared, a facility which is not available for the semi or the repeater. However, I know that many of those who use these guns swear by them and shoot extremely well.

The Over-and-Under Shotgun

There was a time, perhaps a half century or more ago, when the over-and-under shotgun (O/U) was beginning to make an impact on the driven game-shooting scene, having already established itself as a gun of choice amongst a growing band of clay shooters. Its history is curious, for prior to the assemblage of barrels side by side, all double-barrelled guns had their barrels in a superposed position, doubtless because up till then shooters were used to the single-barrel system, which the over-and-under appeared to mimic. It was not until Henry Nock's patent breech in the 1780s enabled flintlock guns to be constructed with shorter and lighter barrels that the side-by-side (S/S) became the norm, leaving the O/U to languish for the best part of a century or more.

In the first quarter of the twentieth century interest in the O/U was revived, largely due to the search by gunmakers for something novel. The side-by-side hammerless ejector had reached its apogee, and such was the longevity of these superb guns that for commercial reasons a new, or revived, type of gun was sought in order to maintain and expand the market. Across the Atlantic the O/U was already well established as a natural cousin to the repeating rifles, such as the Winchester with tubular magazines beneath the barrel and large fore-ends. The O/U shotgun would look similar and feel at home to Americans brought up in the tradition of these rifles.

Today the over-and-under dominates the shooting field.

The renowned writer on all gun matters, Gough Thomas, who edited the very popular 'Gun Gossip' column in *Shooting Times* magazine when I was editor, was not a fan of the O/U. He claimed that it offered no radical improvement on the more popular S/S system, but nevertheless he observed in 1965 that 'most trap shooters and a few game shooters prefer the O/U, and consider that they shoot better with it, which, for them, puts it above all argument'. Gough went on the say that the increasing adoption of the O/U by clay shooters was bound to have a marginal influence on game shooters. Indeed he was right to some extent, though 'marginal' can now be translated into 'all-embracing'!

Today, the O/U has overtaken the S/S in the game-shooting field to such an extent that it is nothing unusual to discover no more than one or two side-by-sides being used in a team of eight Guns by the covert side. An older generation will largely remain loyal to the S/S, through tradition and familiarity, though I know several older shooting men who have chosen to switch to an O/U, often in 20-bore; they prefer the lighter weight and single sighting plane. Indeed, a gun that seems to dominate the driven bird scene is, today, the Beretta O/U 20-bore. It is also a gun that is particularly popular with lady shooters.

Choice of Gun

So back to the choice of a gun. Where the S/S is concerned the beginner can consider a boxlock or sidelock, an ejector or non-ejector, and single or double triggers. Obviously cost is a major factor, but if the pit is bottomless, then in terms of craftsmanship, design and practical purpose, the English-made side-lock hammerless ejector must be a strong contender, followed closely by a quality over-and-under.

All very fine, but for the newcomer to the sport with a limited budget, the answer may well be a sound, well made boxlock, be it English or foreign. First, though, let's clarify the difference between boxlock and side-lock. In the case of the boxlock, the lockwork is set into a solid action body beneath the breech and forward of the trigger guard. Most boxlocks are made on the Anson and Deeley system, which was patented in 1875, and is considered to have resulted in the first really successful hammerless gun.

A side-by-side hammerless boxlock, depending on the price, can have manual extraction of cartridges or selective ejectors, triggers can be single or double, and, indeed, almost any specification can be produced. These guns can range from basic models up to premier grade, and are usually hard-wearing and give little trouble. The very cheap models, however, can feel clumsy and ill-balanced – but then, as in all things, you get what you pay for.

To my old-fashioned way of thinking the hammerless sidelock ejector represents the peak of gunmaking. Yes, I know there are some exquisite over-and-unders on the market, but anyone who picks up a Purdey, a Holland & Holland or a William Evans will know at once that the gun is alive in their hands. The balance, the finish and the sheer artistry place this breed of shotgun in a class of its own. Unfortunately, at that end of the market a second mortgage is often required to own one! However, there are some outstanding sidelocks made in Spain and Italy. My first such a gun was made by AYA, the renowned Spanish firm, and cost, new, £120! With that gun I shot everything from snipe to driven wild boar using solid ball cartridge, and it never let me down. However, it is now owned by someone else, for it was stolen from me at a Game Fair at Harewood House, Leeds.

A sidelock, as opposed to a boxlock, usually achieves an improved degree of balance by virtue of the fact that the lockwork is mounted on removable plates set into the side of the action and is seen as an oval plate set above the trigger guard and in front of the wrist. It is a more expensive and intricate system but it offers a smooth, clean outline and goes a long way towards ensuring excellent balance.

Barrel lengths today are usually about 28in, though there was a time when 30in would have been considered normal. In those far-off days there was a myth circulating in the shooting world that longer barrels shot harder and farther, but this delusion was firmly scotched when, in the 1920s, the renowned gunmaker Robert Churchill introduced to the market a 25in-barrelled gun. The older school of shooting men derided this short-barrelled shotgun, but tunes soon had to be changed when it was shown that for swift snap-shots at driven partridges or, say, teal at dusk, the ease of movement and sheer 'pointability' of the Churchill XXV placed it in a class of its own. It also had the advantage of lightness, an attribute recognized by the older sportsman. However, there are shooting men who claim that the additional 3in of a 'normal' gun's barrel are an aid to killing high overhead pheasants. Not everyone would agree, and the XXV is still regarded by many excellent shots as the ideal in terms of barrel length, weight and balance.

Ejector or non-ejector? Personally I would always opt for an ejector, especially if there is a chance you will be taking part, at some stage, in driven shoots. Having to extract cartridges manually must inevitably slow down the rate of fire, and on a bitterly cold day, when fingers are numb, fumbling to remove empty cases while birds are in the air can be singularly frustrating.

Choke

Now, the scary subject of choke! This can so easily be a trap for the unwary novice. Choke, first of all, is the degree of constriction at the muzzle which compresses the charge of shot as it leaves the barrel, and in so doing, creates a tighter pattern. Imagine holding a hose-pipe in one hand without any compression, but squeeze the end of the hose and where before the jet of water was wide, now it reduces to a narrow jet. It is similar to shot leaving a muzzle. Too often, though, the shooter new to the sport assumes that tight, dense patterns must retain hard-hitting, long-range properties. Armed with a gun carrying full choke in the left barrel and half in the right he fancies himself invincible. Well, yes, he may occasionally pull off an exceptionally long shot, but a snipe zigzagging up from a marsh, a teal flaring skywards or a pigeon drifting over the decoys twenty yards away will either be missed – the most likely outcome – or if hit will be badly smashed and of little use for the kitchen.

The fact of the matter is that full choke makes more demand on aiming accuracy than does quarter choke or cylinder. One should understand that most game is shot at moderate ranges of twenty-five to thirty-five yards, distances at which open-bored guns are more than capable of delivering killing patterns. At these ranges a heavily choked gun will, if the bird is hit, smash it with far too many tightly bunched pellets or, more likely, miss it completely. As previously mentioned, my old hammer-gun by Cogswell & Harrison, which was built in 1878 and has damascus barrels that have gone through proof, delivers superb patterns despite the fact that both barrels are true cylinder.

Too much choke is a snare and a delusion, and for general rough and game shooting I would advocate no more than quarter choke in the right barrel and half choke in the left. Forget full choke, and remember that choke can always be reduced and that good patterns produce good shooting. I would never consider purchasing a gun without knowing how it patterned, and here most reputable gunmakers will have access to a shooting ground where clients can test-fire potential purchases, not only to check fit and feel, but also to see how they perform at the pattern plate with a variety of cartridges.

You can, of course, test pattern a gun yourself provided you have a suitable and safe area to hand. You will require a six-foot (2m) square sheet of metal or wood that can be white-washed and fixed to a stout, firm support. A distance of exactly forty yards (36.58m) should be measured to the point where the shooter stands, and then, using a game load with which the shooter is familiar and happy, a shot is fired at the centre of the plate.

One then selects by eye the centre of the pattern and draws round it a 30in (76cm) circle. Don't just draw a 30in circle and then fire at it, as you are trying to discover *where* your gun shoots as well as the sort of pattern it produces. The pattern should then be judged on uniformity, and the number of pellets within the circle or striking its edge should be counted. Make a note of any empty patches or areas where shot has 'balled' or stuck together. Stand back, take a good look at the pattern, and decide whether you feel it is even and the pellets well distributed. Whitewash the plate and repeat this exercise half-a-dozen times, firing from the same barrel.

Remember, too, that many foreign-made guns imported to Britain often carry far too much choke, though companies, particularly in Spain, who have studied the requirements of the British shooter have long since realized that excessive choke is not required. However, too much choke can always be removed by a competent gunmaker.

The Shotgun Certificate

So, now you are armed with sufficient knowledge to make a tentative decision about the acquisition of your first gun. However, before you can make

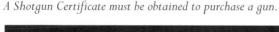

A Shotgun Certificate must be obtained to purchase a gun.

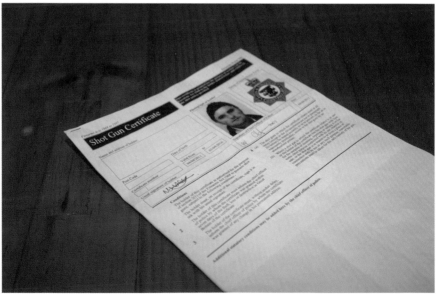

a purchase you must be in possession of a shotgun certificate (SC). This is issued by the Firearms Department of your local constabulary and is also required to be displayed whenever you need to purchase cartridges.

First of all, the definition of a shotgun. It is defined as a smooth-bore gun (not an air rifle), with a barrel not less than 24in (60cm) in length and with a bore not exceeding 2in (5cm) in diameter. It either has no magazine or a non-detachable magazine, which cannot hold more than two cartridges.

To obtain a shotgun certificate the applicant must apply for the necessary form from the Firearms Department of the constabulary in which he or she resides. There are a number of requirements, including passport-type photographs and the endorsement and counter signature of someone who has known the applicant for at least two years and who has a certain standing in the community, such as a member of a professional body, a qualified teacher in a recognized school, or who holds a regular commission in Her Majesty's Forces and who can vouch for his or her suitability to be granted a certificate. Members of one's immediate family are not eligible.

Whilst there are also a number of stipulations with which the grantee must comply, the fact is that an application for a shotgun certificate must be granted to the applicant unless the Chief Officer of Police has reason to believe that the person is a prohibited person with a criminal record (any previous conviction must be revealed on the application form), or is satisfied that the applicant does not have a good reason for possessing, purchasing or acquiring a shotgun.

However, assuming that all the requirements on the application form are met, then the shotgun certificate must be granted to the applicant. Whilst there is no stipulation to say that a security cabinet must be in use, the certificate does stipulate that every reasonable precaution must be made to keep the gun secure. Such a cabinet is, I believe, absolutely essential, and must be secured in the house where it will not be readily discovered. An accessible attic with the cabinet screwed to a wall or other secure fixture is a sensible option, and only, repeat only, the shotgun certificate holder should know where the keys are kept. Not even his wife or partner should be aware of where they are hidden. The current cost of grant of a shotgun certificate is £50 and £40 on renewal.

Once your application is received, a number of routine checks are conducted and you will then be contacted by a Firearms Enquiry Officer who will arrange an appointment with you to discuss the security of your gun(s) and any queries you may have. A certificate, once granted, is valid for five years.

You should also be aware that if you intend at some juncture to take your shotgun to another EC country you will then require a European firearms pass (EFP). This is valid to the date when your SC expires or is to be renewed, a period of three years. There is no fee for this service, and if an EFP is required it can be obtained through your Firearms Licensing Department.

There is no minimum age limit for obtaining a shotgun certificate, but anyone under the age of fifteen and wishing to use a shotgun must be supervised by an adult aged at least twenty-one. From the ages of fifteen to seventeen one may be given a shotgun but cannot buy a gun or cartridges, and it is only at the age of eighteen that one can do both.

There is often some confusion and puzzlement over the status of antique guns. The following do not require a certificate provided they are not fired; if they are, then a shotgun certificate is needed:

- All original muzzle-loading firearms made before 1939
- Breech-loading firearms using ignition systems other than rim-fire or centre-fire, including pin-fire, needle-fire and contemporary transitional ignition systems
- Breech-loading shotguns originally chambered for obsolete cartridges

If your shotgun requires repair then the repairer must examine your shotgun certificate, and similarly, when you wish to purchase shotgun cartridges you must also produce your SC. There are, however, occasions when a person can have a shotgun in their possession and use it without holding an SC. In the first instance, one can use a gun at a time and place approved by the police for shooting artificial targets, and secondly there is an exception, which permits someone to borrow a shotgun from the occupier of private premises and to use it in the presence of the gun's owner on those premises. Both exceptions enable youngsters and complete novices to receive training.

Gun and Cartridge Safety

Gun and cartridge safety at all times, both in and outside the shooting field, is of paramount importance. Guns carried in vehicles must be contained in sleeves or cases and placed in a position where the public cannot readily see them. Cartridges, too, should never be exposed in their boxes or held in belts for the general gaze. Similarly, guns and cartridges must never, at any time, be left in an empty vehicle, be it only for a matter of minutes. Cars can be stolen and broken into, and the loss of a gun and ammunition under these circumstances is likely to lead to a forfeiture of your certificate and possible financial penalties.

Now, let us consider your options when buying a first gun. Money is the key to the exercise and will dictate your approach, but it must also be coupled to caution and wariness. The innocence of youth can lead to some disastrous ventures, as I know only too well. One still occasionally comes across ancient shotguns that are out of proof, with pitted barrels and a shaky action. Such wrecks are fit only to be hung on the wall as a souvenir, and should never, ever be fired: you could easily lose a hand if a barrel bursts.

The Second-Hand Gun

If you are offered a second-hand gun, be it privately or through a dealer, first break it to make sure it is unloaded, and then peer up the barrels, holding them against the light so that any dents, pits or bulges can be detected. Then with a cleaning rod, push a rolled-up piece of tissue through the tubes to remove any oil that might be concealing a small pit or mark. Now reverse the barrels and look through them from the muzzle ends, again checking for any signs of pitting. Minor pitting, normally the outcome of careless cleaning, need not necessarily condemn a gun, and if cared for and cleaned assiduously the gun may well continue to give good service. Dents, usually identified inside the barrel by a half moon reflection, or even felt on the outside of the barrel, can often be taken out by a gunmaker, but a bulge caused by excessive pressure, due perhaps to an obstruction in the barrel when it was fired, at once condemns the gun.

Next, remove the barrels from the action and check the various proof marks that will be found on the flats of the underside of the barrel at the breech end. All shotguns made in Great Britain must have passed tests imposed by the Birmingham and London proof houses, apart from guns from certain countries whose proof regulations are accepted here. It is also illegal to sell, hire or give away any gun that has not been proved and does not possess valid proof marks. Remember, too, that whilst a gun may possess marks to indicate that it passed for nitro-proof, that does not necessarily mean that it is *still* in proof. A great deal of use and excessive wear may have worn away metal in the barrels, placing it outside the category for which it was originally proved. Only a qualified gunmaker, using a special gauge to test the thickness of the barrel walls, can tell whether it is in or out of proof.

It would be most unwise for the novice shooter even to attempt to interpret or rely on the proof markings on a second-hand gun, and he should seek the advice of a reputable gun dealer or gunmaker. If he is buying a gun directly from a dealer then he should be fully protected by the dealer's reputation.

It is a complement to the British gun trade that there are still guns in use today that were made well over a century ago, and which, despite having damascus barrels, have passed nitro-proof despite the fact that they were originally intended solely for black powder. However, to use a gun originally built for black powder with modern nitro cartridges is to court severe injury or even death every time the trigger is squeezed. One has only to examine some of the wrecked guns held at the Birmingham Proof House to see the disastrous effect of using a modern cartridge in a black powder gun, and also the horrific damage caused by an obstruction in the barrel when the gun is fired. One of the constant dangers in this respect is, as mentioned before, the inadvertent insertion of a 20-bore cartridge into a 12-bore chamber, followed by a 12-bore cartridge which is fired. The torn metal would almost certainly cause, at the very least, the loss of a hand.

It is also worth checking the barrels of a second-hand gun to make sure they are steel and not damascus. They may have been newly blacked, but under a strong light one should be able to detect the give-away faint patterning that indicates that the barrels were made from the damascus twist method, which involved literally twisting and welding together a number of steel rods. There were varying degrees of method and rods used, but the results usually produced a barrel with a fine and attractive pattern, and this would normally be browned.

Check the top rib if the gun is a side-by-side, and make sure that it is not loose or that any rust has worked its way under the metal, and perhaps into the barrel. Even hold the barrel up to your ear and listen for any rust trickling up and down the rib. Now replace the barrels to the stock and action, but don't put back the fore-end. Hold the wrist of the stock and move the gun sideways. If there is any indication of shake it means that the action needs tightening. Replace the fore-end and hold the breech up against the light. If the barrels are 'off the face' of the action you will be able to detect light between the breech and the face of the action. In a really bad case, moving the barrels back and forth by the wrist will enable you to see and feel movement in the action.

Today, you are less likely to encounter a gun that has been dolled up for sale, but for the man who knows what he is up to, nothing is simpler than to give a face-lift to a clapped-out wreck. Barrels that are pitted can be lapped out by having metal skimmed away, worn-out chequering can be recut, barrels re-blacked, woodwork polished, dents lifted and a loose action temporarily tightened. Fortunately, today the gun trade is so well regulated and looked after by the exemplary Gun Trade Association that such instances of fraudulent behaviour are indeed rare and never found within the realms of the GTA.

The Outlets for Gun Purchase

So, where and what are the reliable outlets for gun purchase? There are basically four obvious sources: the gunmaker, the gun dealer, the auction house specializing in firearms, and the private seller.

The Gunmaker

Obviously, if money does not call the tune, then one's problem is readily solved through the services of a 'best' London gunmaker. One can have a gun built to one's personal requirements and specifications, fitted, tested and supplied with case and accessories. It will cost a small fortune and probably take a minimum of two or more years to build, but it will be of the finest quality and a potential heirloom, or, at the very least, an investment. A best quality London-made gun, perhaps by Purdey, Holland & Holland, Boss or William Evans, remains a world beater, and whilst foreign gunmakers may try to compete, none carry the cachet attributed to a best English sidelock from a leading maker.

The Gun Dealer

However, let's come back to reality! From a personal point of view, if I were in the market for a new or second-hand gun, whatever its configuration, I would in the first instance consult a reputable gun dealer, especially one who has access to a shooting ground and can either himself fit a gun, or use the services of a professional gunfitter-cum-coach. Such a dealer will have a wide selection of both new and second-hand guns, and should be able to offer impartial advice. He may have the ability and knowledge to make sure that a client handles a gun of his choice which fits, but if he does not, this is where the knowledge of a shooting ground instructor is so invaluable.

Gun Fit

Gun fit is the key to good shooting. I have known game shots who, season after season, and despite paying good money for their sport, remain consistently poor or even hopeless shots. So often their ability to miss or wound birds with remarkable consistency is due entirely to the fact that their guns do not fit. Each of us has a different physical composition. We may be tall and gangly with long arms, or short-armed and stout, or stooped or straight, but in every case we require a gun that meets our physical demands. A stock that is too long or short, or has a drop which forces the handler to lower their head, will ensure that their shooting career will be defined by constant frustration and disappointment.

The beginner seeking a first gun may place himself in the hands of the gun dealer who, naturally, wishes to make a sale, but it is always advisable, under these circumstances, to bring along an experienced friend to offer views and opinions. In the shop the potential purchaser can handle and raise to his shoulder a variety of guns, but it is only on the shooting ground that he can be assured of impartial and professional advice from an instructor. Here he will discover which is his master eye. With the majority of people it is the right eye, and if he is right-handed then there is no problem, but if he has a left master eye and is still right-handed, then complications can arise.

The instructor may use a try-gun, which has a stock that can be altered to fit the physical attributes of the potential buyer. Whatever the method adopted by the instructor, it is absolutely vital that the novice receives the best advice, and can be confident that the gun he likes and feels confident with fits his physical conformation. Furthermore, under these circumstances he or she can also have a shooting lesson with the gun of their choice. Remember that the gun must fit the shooter, rather than the shooter fitting him or herself to the gun.

Alterations may have to be made to the selected gun in order to ensure a perfect fit, and these can be costly unless the gun dealer is prepared to include them in the price of the gun in order to ensure a sale.

All reputable dealers will have a wide selection of second-hand guns for sale. These will have been carefully serviced and will, of course, be in proof. Such guns can often prove excellent value, and even if, after sale, some problem occurs, the gun dealer or shop will normally make sure that it is swiftly rectified.

What about the case for the hammer-gun? Well, I have to admit a certain bias as I have used one of these guns for many years without any problems. There is, I maintain, a particular pleasure in cocking a hammer in anticipation of a shot, and though the hammerless gun is more efficient and faster in use, the hammer-gun was, of course, used extensively by sportsmen until the advent of its hammer-shorn descendant in the late nineteenth century. I certainly would not suggest, for one moment, that this type of gun is suitable for a beginner, as the manipulation of the hammers does require a degree of skill and care. The danger lies in the hammer slipping from the thumb while the hammer is being cocked or uncocked. This action should always be taken with the barrels pointing at the sky and the left hand firmly gripping the barrels. Pointing the gun at the ground while engaging in this action can, in fact, prove dangerous, as the movement is awkward and the thumb may slip over the ear of the hammer.

An increasing number of experienced shots use hammer-guns on occasion, and these guns if in sound condition, nitro-proved and by a good maker, are now fetching substantial sums, when a few years ago they could scarcely be given away. However, they are not, I repeat, suitable for the beginner.

Buying Second-Hand

Buying second-hand privately can be a minefield! Guns may be advertised in the classified columns of the shooting press or offered for sale on a friendly, private basis. In most cases the gun may be perfectly acceptable, but it is very much a case of *caveat emptor*: let the buyer beware. Expert knowledge is required to examine and assess such a gun which, whilst it may on the surface appear to be in good order, can conceal a raft of hidden faults. A seller of integrity should be content to let the would-be purchaser have the gun vetted by a gun dealer or shop, not only for its condition, proof and safety but also for its value.

Guns can also be bought at auction, of course. There are several reputable auction houses that specialize in firearms, and one can be assured that guns offered at auction will have been thoroughly checked to make sure they are in proof and in sound condition. Details of each gun will be found in the catalogue, and usually an indication of the estimated sale price will also be offered. Yet again, the beginner needs to tread extremely warily, and must ensure that he is accompanied by a knowledgeable companion at the pre-auction viewing. Whilst a gun may be acquired at what appears to be a reasonable, or better than reasonable, knock-down price, one must also cost in the fact that the gun may need subsequently to be fitted and possibly require alterations. However, bargains can be found in this market, but caution is the key word.

Cartridges

Now, the question of cartridges! I have to confess that, as a result of years of shooting a wide variety of quarry, I have long since reduced my cartridges requirements to a state of simplicity! I am not, nor ever have been, a ballistician and, frankly, have not the slightest interest in loading my own cartridges or producing special loads. At the end of the day I need only know the bore size, the load I require and the size of shot.

There was a time long ago, when as a confirmed wildfowler I was committed to a heavily choked, 3in chambered Greener 12-bore weighing in
the region of 8lb. It was a monster, with that horrid side-safety beloved of
Greener. I even painted the barrels grey! I was, I fancied, the archetypal
wildfowler, and it was only after a number of relatively fruitless outings,
including one flight on a rising tide in Chichester Harbour when I managed
to down three teal for thirty shots, that the penny dropped: if I had been
using a lighter gun with, say, half choke and improved or even cylinder, I
would have gone home with a very heavy side-bag.

The fact of the matter is that today the factory-loaded cartridge meets
all requirements – apart from cost! The sportsman with a 2½in chambered 12-bore game gun, weighing between 6¼lb and 7lb, has a choice of
four shot loads, namely 28gm (1oz), 30gm (1⅟₁₆oz), 32gm (1⅛oz) and 34gm
(1¼oz). However, the majority of game and rough-shooting shots will stick
to 28gm or 30gm loads in No. 6 or No. 7 shot size. A 30gm load of No. 6 shot
will contain 287 pellets, a load that will deal more than adequately with the
majority of situations that arise in the shooting field.

With experience the shooter may reduce or increase this load to 28gm
or 32gm. Pigeons coming in over decoys may call for no more than 28gm
of No. 6 or 7 shot, but if they are flighting in to roost, perhaps with a wind
behind them, then the load could be upped to 30gm of No. 6. Many years
ago a myth circulated that wood pigeon were protected by their feathers and
that heavy shot, such as No. 5, was required to penetrate their body armour.
It was a legend that possibly arose because pigeons shed feathers all too readily, and some shooters swore that when a bird flew away leaving a few feathers floating in the air it had been hard hit, whereas it was more likely that a
stray pellet had dislodged a tuft of feathers.

There are, of course, occasions when the shot load needs to be more
readily attuned to the intended quarry. I would not, for instance, set out
on a goose flight with a belt full of cartridges loaded with 30gm of No. 6
shot, or walk up snipe with 32gm of No. 4! Geese are big, powerful birds
that demand an appropriate cartridge response. Yes, a goose hit in the head
at twenty-five or thirty yards will be quite dead, but hit in the body with
this load it will carry on, perhaps to drop, badly wounded, a mile away.
Geese, especially those shot below the sea wall, call for a heavy load such as
1¼oz of No. 1 or BB. Inland, when shot at over decoys, No. 3 or No. 4 shot
may be appropriate. In this case a 3in 12-bore magnum is the tool to do the
business.

However, the new entrant to the shooting scene will almost certainly spend his or her apprenticeship years in the game-shooting field,

supplemented by some pigeon shooting and modest wildfowling outings. A well fitted 12-bore side-by-side or over-and-under, with reasonably open chokes and serviced with 28gm or 30gm of No. 6 or 7, will accommodate most occasions. Opinions will differ and there are experienced shots who maintain that to shoot snipe successfully, for instance, very small shot such as No. 8 is essential. Well, maybe, but I have shot both walked-up and driven snipe with No. 6. If the pattern is placed correctly the result will be a dead bird.

I have little interest in loading my own cartridges or delving too deeply into the esoteric world of ballistics, yet I know that for some shooters this is an arena filled with exciting possibilities. For my part, I prefer to rely on factory-loaded cartridges and have had no cause to regret this over the years.

The Use of Lead Shot and its Alternatives

Without question lead shot is the most effective and efficient charge in a cartridge, but today, since the then Government signed the African-Eurasian Waterbird Agreement in November 1999, lead shot has been proscribed in various situations as a result of claims that waterfowl were being poisoned by the ingestion of spent lead shot. Claims, I might add, that have been the subject of both dispute and exaggeration. However, the law is the law and must be complied with.

How does it affect shooting in Britain? Well, in England, regulations ban the use of lead shot over all areas of the foreshore, over specified Sites of Special Scientific Interest (SSSIs), and for the shooting of all ducks, geese, coots and moorhens wherever they are found. The Welsh Assembly imposed similar restrictions from 1 September 2002.

The system in Scotland is based around the RAMSAR definitions of wetland. The RAMSAR Convention is an international agreement signed in Ramsar, Iran, in 1971 relating to wetlands of international importance. As far as Scotland is concerned, the use of lead shot over any area of wetland is proscribed for any shooting activity. Wetlands are defined as, regardless of size, any areas of foreshore, marsh, fen, peatland with standing water, regularly or seasonally flooded fields and other sources, man-made or natural, static or flowing, fresh, brackish or salt. In other words, wherever there is water, lead shot is banned.

In Northern Ireland restrictions on the use of lead shot were put in place from 1 September 2009 and are based on the Scottish approach.

Whether or not shooters agree with these stipulations is irrelevant. This is the law, and as such it must be obeyed. However, there is not the slightest doubt that whilst coastal wildfowlers rigorously adhere to the restrictions on the use of lead, it would appear that some inland duck and goose shooters are flouting the law. In 2002 it was shown that two-thirds of duck sampled at game dealers countrywide had been shot with lead. Wildfowlers invariably retain any duck or geese they shoot, usually in very small numbers, for their personal use. However, there are inland game shoots, commercial and private, which may include duck, reared or wild, in the bag, and the majority of these are disposed of to game dealers.

This behaviour is intolerable, and unless there is a swift change of heart, there is a possibility that lead shot could be banned across the board. If such a political and unjustified step were to be taken, the cost of shooting would rise due to the soaring costs of alternatives to lead, whilst in addition many older English guns would be consigned to the scrap-heap. Modern 'best' guns are now designed to be compatible with steel shot, and whilst a small number of older guns can be modified to accept steel by reducing choke constriction and lengthening cartridge chambers, these are very few, and no steel loads are available for 2½in chambers. Older guns, which often have thin barrel walls, may be damaged if steel shot is used. Alternatives such as tungsten or bismuth may be considered acceptable for older classic guns, but these cartridges are ridiculously expensive. At the time of writing, 'improved bismuth' is £25.50 for a box of twenty-five cartridges, and 'tungsten matrix' is £27.50 a box. However, it is claimed that tungsten matrix is safe to use in older guns, and is almost as effective as lead.

On a personal note I have used steel shot when duck shooting and have found it to be vastly inferior to lead. Birds flying at thirty to forty yards were seldom killed outright but usually wounded, and this was not just as a result of inadequate shooting on my part, but was the general finding of a party of experienced Guns in my party. Tin shot was also once advocated but made no impression, almost literally! I tried it out on walked-up pheasants and discovered that whilst a puff of feathers might depart from a bird at twenty or so yards, there was no other ill effect as far as the pheasant was concerned.

So at the end of the day, one must hope that lead shot remains legal and available for game shooting and pigeon control. It is highly efficient, kills cleanly, and is, without question, the best option available. Opponents to its use, such as the RSPB and the Wildfowl and Wetlands Trust, hope that a ban on lead for all types of bird shooting might lead to a long-term destruction of the sport as a result of the escalating cost of alternatives. Claims, too, that lead shot in game can result in lead poisoning are patently absurd. Thousands of sportsmen and women have eaten game throughout their lives with absolutely no ill effect.

4
Clothing and Equipment

Let's take a glance back in time to see how shooters have coped in the shooting field. When we look back at prints of sportsmen in the eighteenth and early nineteenth centuries there is a sense of wonderment and almost disbelief that our sporting ancestors braved the field in tricornes, wideawakes or top hats, drab buttoned-up leggings and full-skirted coats and waistcoats. Greens and browns may have been chosen, but little attention was paid to the concept of garments that were of practical use in the field. The shooting man's outfit was little more than an adaptation of his normal daytime dress, and it was not until the middle of the nineteenth century, and thence onwards, that shooting men began to adapt their dress to the practical needs of the field.

Plus-fours, breeches, leather and cloth gaiters, leather boots and spats became increasingly worn by all classes as the nineteenth century headed up to the twentieth. Photographs of shooting parties in the late nineteenth and the early years of the following century disclose a fairly standard style of dress amongst game shooters: a tweed jacket, often with a waistcoat, plus-fours or plus-twos of the same material, wool stockings and leather boots or even shoes, and the whole topped by either a tweed cap or a soft hat such as a trilby, completed the outfit for the field.

A photograph of the renowned ballistician and shooting man, Sir Ralph Payne Gallwey, posing in his shooting room, shows him wearing an outfit that would pass in today's game-shooting field without comment.

The Game Shooter of the Twenty-First Century

However, the game shooter of the twenty-first century has the enormous advantage over his ancestors of modern fabrics that are water- and windproof, comfortable, and perfectly acceptable in the shooting field. So-called Norfolk jackets bearing a belt at the rear are still occasionally seen, but there is little to compare with a three-piece tweed outfit incorporating plus-twos rather than their baggy fore-runners, plus-fours. Worn with a shirt and tie, plain green or brown socks and stout leather boots, this ensemble takes some

Today's game shooters have a wide choice of clothing.

beating. It should be topped with a flat cap or, my preference, a brown trilby. This outfit will repel the elements and keep the wearer warm and comfortable. In the wettest and most chilling weather a waterproof, of which there are dozens of types on the market today, can be worn, or always kept handy in a vehicle or the shoot bus.

It is worth ensuring that plus-twos fit firmly just below the knee. Some use Velcro as a fastener, others have buttons, but whatever the method adopted it must ensure that the breeches are held firmly in place. Nothing looks worse than loose plus-twos and wrinkled socks!

I am no fan of the fashion for garishly coloured wool socks and always think, probably without any justification, that they tend to denote the newcomer to the shooting field who, for some obscure reason, feels he must draw attention to himself. Wear green or brown socks with matching garters, which are used to hold up the socks.

Tweed is still unmatched in terms of warmth and protection, and it is little wonder that it is the garment of choice of the stalker in Scotland, whether professional or amateur. The jacket, however, must be quite loosely cut to accommodate the wearer's ability to use a gun, so there is plenty of 'give' in it when he swings at a bird or prepares for a shot with a rifle. Nothing is worse than a jacket that constricts movement.

Another cloth that is quite outstanding in terms of warmth and protection from rain and wind is lodencloth. Made from untreated sheep's wool, this type of jacket, usually in green, is popular on the Continent, particularly amongst stalkers. I wore such a jacket for years and found it to be almost unbeatable. It's only weakness lay in the fact that the surface tension had to be maintained. In other words, leaning one's elbow on a hard, wet surface could cause a seepage.

Whilst the tweed cap, in its various guises, is seen as the normal head-gear for the covert-side, one occasionally comes across a Gun wearing a deer-stalker. Although seen by some as somewhat quaint, these hats do have the advantage of ear-flaps, which can be loosened to button under the chin. On a bitter day with a freezing wind this is not to be sneezed at! One form of head covering that should never be seen in the shooting field is the polo-type cap. Beloved of Americans, it has no place on the British shooting scene.

Cold, chilled hands also have to be considered. Few things are worse than blue fingers which can barely move to break open a gun – but there are a number of safeguards. Pocket hand warmers are well worth considering, and can keep one's hand in good order between shots. Personally, I cannot wear thick woollen gloves on a shooting day, though there are gloves on the market in a warm, modern fabric, which are thin and also have a fore-finger that can be turned back on itself and attached with Velcro so that the finger is free to squeeze the trigger. I have never found woollen mitts with fingertips missing of any use whatsoever, nor have wool-lined wristbands been of any practical value in keeping one's hands warm. Silk-lined gloves made from the finest and thinnest of leathers are only moderately useful in chilly weather, but when it rains they are quite useless.

The covert side demands a reasonable degree of smartness, combined with protection against the elements. The keepers will themselves set the standard, wearing estate tweeds on the smartest shoots, but whatever the status of the shoot they will turn themselves out smartly and neatly dressed for the day. On all driven days a tie is obligatory, and nothing looks worse or sloppier than an open-neck shirt. It's not a question of snobbishness, but simply setting a standard.

Cartridges

A minor transgression of the driven day is to run out of cartridges during a drive, and you can be absolutely sure that the birds will all make a beeline for the silent peg! Rushing round to try and beg cartridges from neighbouring

Cartridge belt with enclosed loops.

Guns can be extremely annoying for all concerned, while the fact that one has not brought sufficient cartridges is an insult to one's host. The answer is, of course, a capacious cartridge bag, and if thought necessary, a back-up supply in the shoot vehicles. Personally, I always wear a cartridge belt in addition to a bag, as I prefer to reload from this source, while cartridges can be slightly raised from the loops for easy access. I dislike carrying cartridges in my pockets as they make the jacket lopsided and are inclined to drag at the shoulders.

On the subject of cartridge belts, I am not a fan of the simple loop type of belt, as cartridges tend to slide through them to the edge of the head case, making it difficult to extract them in a hurry. Instead I have an all-leather belt with four separate pouches, with the base of each loop enclosed so that a sufficient length of cartridge is exposed for easy extraction. However, I have to confess that this is a one-off, though an item that could readily be made by a leather worker.

A shooting stick is definitely a useful adjunct, and if you do decide to purchase one, make sure it has a broad leather seat. There is also on the market a seat that doubles as a magnetic-tipped empty cartridge case collector. For those of us who are of an advanced age, this can be extremely useful!

Clothing and Equipment on the DIY Shoot

The development of the DIY shoot, a phenomenon that has really taken off in recent years, has created a very different scenario to the formal game shoot regarding clothing and equipment. The great majority of small DIY shoots operate on the basis of minimum costs, and as a result, shooting takes place on a stand and walk basis. In other words, beaters are not employed, and instead the Guns, of whom there will usually be in the region of sixteen to eighteen, divide into standing and beating teams for each drive.

Under these circumstances a more informal and practical approach to clothing and equipment is demanded. You may be standing for one drive, and then having to negotiate thick cover, brambles, ditches and wire on the next. Plus-twos and rubber boots, or the leather and canvas-type boots that are so popular, will suit your purpose, and you can, of course, always wear waterproof and thornproof over-trousers, half or full length. In other words, clothing and gear must be able to adapt to the two roles of shooting and beating.

Today there is such an extensive variety of clothing to choose from that the shooting man is almost spoilt for choice. Leaving aside tweed suits, suitable for the driven game scene, modern technology has created a raft of sporting clothing that is wind- and rainproof, in most cases lightweight, with well designed pockets. Some jackets have integral hoods, which can be unrolled, but these are, in my opinion, only for extreme emergency use. I find that wearing a hood is nothing but a hindrance: one cannot see or hear comfortably, and somehow the wretched thing always becomes twisted or collapses at a critical moment.

Shooting Jackets

Over the years I have owned a variety of shooting jackets. When I first started my shooting career I spent most of my time on the foreshore clad in an ex-parachute smock. Practical, camouflaged and warm, its only drawback was the fact that it was only partially waterproof. I bought it in an army surplus store in Aldershot for a fiver! If only I'd kept it, for these smocks now make serious money and very occasionally come up on eBay.

From the para smock I shifted to the famous Barbour's Solway smock constructed from oiled Egyptian cotton. These jackets, in various guises, were the making of the Barbour company, and for many years dominated the shooting and country sports field. Even today, ancient Barbour jackets still occasionally appear, worn by proud owners reluctant to dustbin this archaic garment. It was totally waterproof and kept out the wind, but there were several drawbacks: in cold weather the garment became so stiff and rigid that one could almost prop it up, but worst of all it did not 'breathe', as I discovered on one occasion when I wore the jacket while deer stalking in Scotland. By the time I had climbed the side of a mountain I was dripping with sweat.

New breathable materials and a multiplicity of designs have filled the market for the past forty or more years, with leading brand names vying with each other to produce the 'ultimate' in shooting apparel. There is, in fact, such a wealth and variety of garments on the market that today's shooter is almost overwhelmed for choice. He can select from fleece jackets, gilets, waistcoats, jerseys, all branded by top and renowned names.

Personally, I have always been inclined to keep my shooting clothing and kit to the bare essentials, and wear only those that have stood the test of time. For the past ten or more years, for game shooting, for picking-up and for stalking, I have worn just one jacket. Made in Finland by a company called Sasta 64 degrees Northern Latitude it is, without question, the best shooting jacket I have ever owned. Lightweight, built from a soft material, which is totally water- and windproof, it is lined with silver-coloured material under black netting. In summer, when I use it for stalking, the jacket remains cool, but in the winter it provides warm protection against the worst weather. In addition, it has soft leather across the shoulders and top of the back. This may not be the best jacket on the market, but without doubt this Finnish family company, founded in 1969, know how to provide protection against the worst the outdoors can throw at you.

Waterproof Over-Trousers

Waterproof over-trousers are absolutely essential if you are beating, picking up, or rough or DIY shooting, and even on a formal driven day, if it is tipping down with rain, then a pair of over-trousers will provide protection. Avoid nylon, which rustles and is no protection against thorns, but go for a stout waxed cotton or something similar. These trousers can be full length or half length, and usually button down the side. Used in conjunction with gaiters, which are now so popular, you will be able to handle the worst cover and the thickest brambles.

Headgear

Where headgear is concerned, on the less formal shoot it is more a matter of comfort and protection, and although many Guns choose a flat tweed cap, others may opt for a fire-and-aft. However, avoid a hat with a long peaked brim as it will tend to cut off your vision when flighting pigeons or duck. Whatever the choice, do not, under any circumstances, go bare-headed into the field because the sight of your face, handsome though it may be, will frighten every living creature in sight.

This brings me to face masks. Personally I cannot abide them, as I find that the gauze draped round one's head is a constant irritant and a deterrent to crisp shooting. Also the mask has a tendency to twist or slip so that every time you move your head an eye-hole ends up under an ear! However, many wildfowlers and pigeon shooters would feel that their outfit was incomplete unless their facial features were masked.

Camouflage

This brings me to the controversial subject of camouflage. Today's stalker, pigeon shooter, rough shooter and wildfowler have each been the subject of a massive advertising onslaught, initially emanating from America. We are assured that unless the sportsman looks like a walking bush or tree then he really has no chance of success in the field: the result is that camouflage outfits, ranging from trousers, shirts, jackets, hats, gloves and even camouflaged gun and rifle stocks, are seen on all sides. One has only to attend a country fair in the height of the summer to get the full picture. For some unknown reason some sportsmen feel it is incumbent to adorn themselves in full camouflage uniform, even under a blazing sun. I sometimes wonder whether these good folk have camouflaged wall and lavatory paper at home! However, that's their choice, but it is one which, I believe, is quite unnecessary.

I recall that years ago, Major Archie Coats, who was a professional pigeon shot, killing in the region of 20,000 birds a year, wore a tweed jacket, pullover, breeches and a floppy hat. Camouflage clothing never came within his orbit and yet he outwitted pigeon on a scale that till then had never before been seen. For my part, I've shot a good few pigeons over decoys and flighting, but have always found that neutral clothing blending into the background has worked perfectly well. Again, in the deer-stalking field only the amateur and beginner will think it necessary to turn out looking like a moving bush. Blending in with the background by wearing green and keeping still are the secrets to success in the field.

So if you feel more comfortable in camouflage gear, that's your choice, but I simply do not believe that it is necessary on the scale promoted by some companies. Perhaps the most ridiculous garment of all is the so-called 'gillie suit', which consists of a hairy garment designed to make the shooter resemble a small moving haystack or a yeti. One can only speculate on the terror and anguish an encounter at dusk would induce in an innocent walker! So much of this gear is designed to make the shooter believe that it is essential to resemble a hedge or the bark of a tree if he is to have any hope of outwitting pigeons, rabbits, deer or whatever, but it simply isn't so!

I have sat under a hedge on a grassy slope shooting rabbits with my .22 rimfire with a silencer. A green shirt, brown trousers and a trilby to shade my face were all that was needed for a bag of a dozen or so bunnies. I long ago learnt this lesson when plains game hunting in southern Africa. In dense bush country wear a dark green shirt and trousers, and where the cover is sparse or mainly thorn, a sandy-coloured outfit will suffice. Complicated camouflage leaf patterns are simply a waste of time and money.

Clothing for the Wildfowler

How about the wildfowler? A degree of warmth and total protection against wet and cold are essentials, and once below the sea wall you are in a totally alien environment. However, whilst you need to be prepared to meet the elements at their worst through the winter months and into February, in September and October wildfowling can be warm, mild and positively hot!

However, let's look at the cold and wet weather gear you will require. Insulation is essential and the key to comfort and warmth. String vests and tights are to be highly recommended; stouter versions of the female garment can be obtained and they are worth every penny. I even wear tights on bitterly cold game-shooting days under breeches. Tough trousers are essential, and I recommend a browse through the contents of an army surplus store. I have a pair of ex-NATO trousers which are ideal for wildfowling and stalking, with drawstrings at the ankle. A long-tailed flannel shirt and a thick sweater with a roll-top neck come next, while today there are insulated waistcoats to add extra warmth. You can also benefit from a waterproof neck-wrap, which will help keep you dry and warm.

Waders

Fishermen's long rubber waders are still worn by the majority of wildfowlers, though all-in-one suits are also on the market, suitably disguised for a

Waders are essential wear for the wildfowler.

marshland background. However, if you choose waders, make sure they are long and have loops so you can attach them to your belt to stop them being sucked off in deep mud. The fit of your waders is critical. Remember you will also be wearing thick woollen socks and, possibly, slip-ons to ensure warm feet. If the boot is tight you will suffer, but on the other hand if the foot is too large you may find the boots being dragged off even though they are looped to your belt.

If you look after your waders they will see you through several seasons: always make sure they are dried inside when you return from an outing by stuffing them with crumpled newspaper and leaving them in a dry and warm room, but not near a fire. Place a long stick inside each boot so that it can dry upside down without touching the ground. When buying waders don't skimp on quality, but purchase the best you can afford.

Headgear

Headgear is critical. Tweed caps and trilbies or deerstalkers are out of place, and basically useless on the marsh. I recommend a balaclava-type helmet or a round tweed hat, which will sit firmly on the head and resist any wind, however strong. You can also use a hood attached to your jacket if the weather is really evil, but I have always found that there is a degree of discomfort and annoyance when you try to turn your head sideways.

A pair of binoculars is essential for the wildfowler.

Jacket

Your jacket must be water- and windproof, and ideally a muddy brown colour. Waxproof jackets are still encountered on the foreshore and there is a great deal to be said for them; tough and totally protective, the old Solway jacket, despite its shortcomings in the field, was long considered the ideal protective covering for the wildfowler.

Gloves

How about gloves? Nothing is worse or more frustrating and painful in bitter winter weather than to find your bare hands so cold and frozen that you can hardly move the safety catch on the gun. Some form of glove is the only real answer, though macho wildfowlers will claim that the real answer is to dip your hands in cold water when you set out for the flight, to inure them to the cold. I have tried this remedy and found it absolutely useless! Thin leather gloves, even when lined, quickly become wet and soggy, sheepskin wrist bandoliers may keep your wrist warm but nothing else, while woollen gloves have no protection against the wet, and mittens with the finger ends removed will guarantee warm hands and frozen finger-tips! The only pair of gloves I own, which do work, are camouflaged with Velcro wrist straps and are lined with thinsulate. They offer really warm protection and the right trigger finger can be bent backwards, again to stick to the glove with Velcro, allowing the fore-finger to operate the trigger.

However, today's shooting market has a wide selection of gloves to meet every need, and both Barbour and Musto offer gloves which, even though they are not cheap, are robust, warm and wet-proof.

Equipment for the Wildfowler

As far as equipment is concerned, the wildfowler must be self-sufficient. There will be occasions when he is on his own in weather conditions which can at best give cause for concern, and at worst be thoroughly dangerous. There is, however, no need to resemble an Arctic explorer or burden your-self with excessive baggage.

The first essential is a reliable, sturdy compass, which you know how to use. You may find no use for it for ten seasons, but sure as fate, one day you're going to be caught out in a sea fret, way out on the mud. Nothing can be more frightening if you are unable to determine whether you are walking back to the sea wall or out to sea.

Most wildfowlers below the sea wall are well aware that mud can be highly treacherous. Not only can it trap the unwary, but it can also plaster you and, far worse, become lodged in your gun barrels. A slight slip in the ooze and both barrels are blocked with blobs of The Wash or Morcambe Bay. You can almost guarantee that this mishap will occur in the middle of the best flight of the season. You're miles from the nearest trees where you might find a stick straight enough to clear the tubes, and you certainly can't hook the mud out with your fingers. A foolish wildfowler might try to shoot the mud out, but the result will be bulged barrels or even no fingers. The answer, however, is simple: always carry a four-piece cleaning rod and a wad of cotton wool or even newspaper. The rods can be held together with a stout rubber band and dropped into the bottom of your side-bag.

A tough waterproof torch is also essential, with spare batteries and bulbs. Obviously you will wear a watch and will have consulted the local tide-table. When setting out to make your way across mudflats or along the sea wall, carry your gun in a slip, which can be tucked away in your side-bag or back-pack when you settle down for a flight. My own preference in the days when I was seriously wildfowling was a roomy back-pack with broad straps, which didn't cut into one's shoulders, and it is surprising just how much kit it will hold.

Apart from personal fuel in the way of food and a thermos of soup or coffee, you will want to consider including a small portable seat, which is not going to sink into the mud. The late Tim Sedgwick, a former editor of *Shooting Times*, developed what he called 'the stool of justice': this consisted of two flat, rectangular boards connected by a short metal tube, screwing into sockets; the height could be adjusted and the seat swivelled. It was ideal for mud and did not take up a lot of room. You may also wish to carry half-a-dozen soft rubber duck decoys, which will require weights and line to anchor them.

I can still recall with faint nostalgia the era of paper cartridges. Older readers will remember the varnished cases and their distinctive smell, but whilst efficient and pleasant to use, they were always subject to the hazard of rain and damp. This was always a potential problem on the marsh or mudflats when a sudden slip and immersion could mean soaked and ruined ammunition. The advent of plastic cartridges transformed the entire shooting scene and eliminated any problems associated with water.

As far as carrying cartridges is concerned, normally a belt of twenty-five and a few extra in your pockets should suffice, though if you anticipate a substantial flight you can always carry a box in your pack.

You may also want to add to your burden by including some lightweight camouflage netting and extendable poles, which can be collapsed into short lengths, to support it. How about using an umbrella painted with camouflage patterns to blend in with the marsh? All you have to do is erect the brolly and ram the handle in the mud, sit behind it and peer through a slit. I never pursued this notion, nor have I ever seen a wildfowler trotting along the sea wall with a rolled-up umbrella, but the idea does, I suggest, have some merit.

There is a great deal more to say on the wildfowling theme, so let's move on to the next chapter.

5
Wildfowling Past and Present

In my book, true wildfowlers can claim their right to the title only by virtue of their presence below the sea wall; on the inland side they become duck and goose shooters. This is a somewhat arbitrary definition, but the inland flight pond shooter cannot, by any stretch of the imagination, call himself a true wildfowler, and the same applies to the man decoying geese on inland fields.

The dedicated wildfowler tends to be a man apart. Self-reliant, and at his most content when by himself under a vaulting sky on the open, wide-stretching mudflats below the sea wall, he will enjoy his game and pigeon shooting inland, but will always find himself drawn to a landscape known only to a dedicated few.

It is some few years now since I last shot below the sea wall, but the years when I haunted the mudflats of Chichester Harbour and The Wash are etched on my memory. The pursuit of duck on inland floods can be a tiring and arduous business and the rewards can often be negligible, but this is not wildfowling, while duck shooting on driven game shoots doesn't come anywhere near the designation.

The true wildfowler will spend as much time as he is able below the sea wall: the iodine smell of seaweed on the tide-line, the plaintive cry of gulls and waders, the sheer thrill of hearing the cackle of distant geese and the sight of a pack of wigeon or teal hurtling across the glistening mudflats – all this is a part of a world of its own, and the pre-dawn rising, the late nights, the cold, and the wet and aching limbs will remain only as a reminder of a sport which is, in its own fashion, unique.

The History of Wildfowling

The background and history of wildfowling in Britain is almost as old as time itself. For centuries wildfowl were hunted for the table, and doubtless our ancestors pursued them with slings and stones, with snares, nets, arrows and firearms, while the trapping of ducks on a commercial scale, using decoy ponds and pipes, lasted right through the nineteenth century and into the twentieth, the last decoy pipe being shut down in the 1960s. Today there is still a scattering of decoy ponds whose funnels take their annual quota of fowl, but these are ringed and released for conservation purposes.

Wildfowling as we know it today was 'invented' by one man, Colonel Peter Hawker who was born in London on 4 December 1786 and who served in Portugal and Spain during the Napoleonic wars, retiring from active service in 1813 as a result of a severe wound received at the battle of Talavera in 1809. It was an injury that was to plague him for the remainder of his life.

Long regarded in shooting circles as 'the father of wildfowling', Hawker's exploits can be assessed in his diary, which can still be found in facsimile reprints. Anyone who has read Hawker's diary will marvel at his tenacity and determination, which placed him so far in advance of contemporary sportsmen. Hawker's love and understanding of wildfowling was largely nurtured on the south coast in Poole Harbour and nearby estuaries where he employed his gun punt. Not noted for his tolerance, time and again he records having potential shots with the big gun ruined by some 'rascal in a canoe' or 'tit-shooter popping away on the shore'. Indeed, it seems that Hawker had much to complain of, for in the early years of the nineteenth century the foreshore was swarming with gunners who shot at anything that flew, and who were not averse to taking pot shots at punt gunners.

As the century advanced, so wildfowling as a sport, rather than as a means of marketing birds, gathered momentum. These were the days of the so-called gentlemen gunners, many of whom were avid bird collectors, seeking rare and unusual specimens. Their activities led to the development of professional guides who earned their living from would-be wildfowlers and the bird collectors.

By the last quarter of the nineteenth century the foreshore swarmed with gunners, wildfowlers, bird collectors and what we would today term marsh cowboys, whose only interest lay in shooting gulls, guillemots and, indeed, anything that flew, in range or out.

Wildfowling Under Threat

By the end of the century it had become obvious to those who had the interest of birds at heart – whether conservationists as we would now term them, or responsible shooting men – that some form of control would have to be exerted to try and ensure that the indiscriminate slaughter of birds for trophy cases and the free-for-all on the foreshore was brought under a degree of reasonable control. If the situation was allowed to continue unchecked, genuine wildfowlers would see their sport brought to an end by the more rabid protectionist lobby.

It was indeed fortunate that two men were at hand to act as saviours of the sport of wildfowling. One was Sir Ralph Payne Gallwey, a leading sportsman and a gentleman wildfowler who pursued the sport countrywide. He was also a noted author, whose third volume of his *Letters to Young Shooters*, published in 1896, is still regarded as one of the finest books on the subject.

The other was a foreshore gunner, Stanley Duncan, who came from a long line of wildfowlers and who lived in Hull. Intelligent and energetic, Duncan spent his formative years shooting on the foreshore and inland, and while as a young man he was indiscriminate with regard to what he slew, killing owls, kingfishers and gulls as well as more conventional quarry, he was aware that pressure on his sport was building. Capable of writing, he began to contribute to *The Shooting Times* magazine, amongst other sporting periodicals, and soon achieved a reputation as an enthusiastic and forward-thinking sportsman.

The Creation of WAGBI

By the early years of the twentieth century Duncan, realizing the dangers that now faced his beloved sport, began to formulate his ideas for an association of wildfowlers for defence and promotion. He had already met Payne Gallwey, who would prove to be an invaluable ally, and in 1907 Duncan wrote to the editor of *The Shooting Times* seeking the magazine's support for a wildfowlers' association. A year later, in March 1908, the first committee meeting of the Wildfowlers' Association of Gt Britain & Ireland (WAGBI) was held in Hull, and shortly after, on 2 April, the first general meeting took place at the Imperial Hotel, Hull (since demolished).

Inevitably, World War I virtually brought further progress to an end. In the 1930s a substantial attack on wildfowling as a sport was launched, and although the sport survived, the opening and closing dates for the shooting season were curtailed. Once again, World War II resulted in a temporary setback for WAGBI. However, by 1950 the Association had five affiliated clubs and a suitcase crammed with files! Seven years later a part-time secretary was appointed to the Association: his name was John Anderton. A former naval officer, Anderton was a commanding, forthright man who worked and played hard, and had the ability to get on with people from every background. It is no exaggeration to say that John Anderton brought WAGBI into the twentieth century and was, in many ways, a major player in the world of field sports and in their protection and promotion.

Anderton understood that if shooting in all its forms, and not just wild-fowling, was to thrive, it would have to co-exist with conservation bodies such as the RSPB. It was fortuitous that he was able to work closely with the then secretary of that organization, Philip Brown, who later was to become editor of *The Shooting Times*. A happy liaison!

The Creation of BASC

On Saturday, 6 June 1981, an annual general meeting of WAGBI was held at Eaton Hall, home of the Duke of Westminster; it was attended by 102 members. The main subject on the agenda was a change of title. It had long been felt that WAGBI, as such, did not cater for anyone other than wildfowlers, and in order to expand, a fresh approach was required. A proposal was put forward suggesting a change of title to 'The British Association for Shooting and Conservation'. The resolution was put to the meeting and carried by eighty-five votes to seventeen, and so, despite the title's resemblance to a Basque separatist movement, BASC entered the shooting arena.

Despite the fact that a firm assurance was given that the interests of wild-fowlers would remain a priority, a number of clubs, notably in the eastern counties, nevertheless took umbrage at the fact that WAGBI had now, to all intents and purposes, been wiped off the map. Several clubs chose to depart from BASC, and whilst one can to some extent understand their ire, this was not a wise move.

Looking back over the years I now think that such was the loyalty to WAGBI amongst wildfowlers (and many of the older brigade still proudly sport their original WAGBI badges), it would have been a shrewd and wise move on the part of BASC to have incorporated WAGBI into the overall structure. Wildfowling could still have been administered from within the BASC structure under its original title, and the sense of continuity could have been maintained.

Today there are scores of well organized wildfowling clubs countrywide, many of whom have now wisely bought their own land. One such is the thriving Kent WA, which owns a great deal of marshland, and the Devon WA, which acquired ground in the Exe estuary, for the purposes of both shooting and conservation.

It is well worth reflecting that had wildfowling clubs not come into existence in the 1950s, with WAGBI to support and guide them through the many problems and pitfalls associated with shooting on the foreshore, then wild-fowling today would be history. There is little doubt that the sport had got out of hand in the years after the last war. Gunners crowded the Wash and the Solway in pursuit of the grey geese and shot at birds that were way out of range. Once on and beyond the sea wall, many became a law unto themselves, shooting at gulls and protected shelduck, and drawing down on themselves the anger of responsible shooting men, not to mention conservationists.

Wildfowling Today

Today, the sport of wildfowling is relatively secure, thanks to all the work at parliamentary and local level which, under WAGBI and BASC, has been undertaken over the years by selfless but determined men, such as the late John Anderton, his successor John Swift, now retired, and many more. Wildfowling still remains an essentially solitary sport, but the lone unclubable wildfowler is now a relic of the past. The wildfowling club structure controls sport on the foreshore, and any newcomer to the sport, if he is serious, must join a club and adhere to its rules.

The days of a 'free-for-all' on the foreshore are long since gone, expunged by the need to exert a sense of responsibility and to co-operate with other users including bird-watchers, yachtsmen, anglers and, of course, the general public. Fortunately, wildfowlers normally operate at unsocial hours and clashes are rare. Wildfowling still remains a solitary sport pursued by single-minded, dedicated sportsmen, but newcomers may find themselves on a waiting list to join a club, and even when accepted, they will have an apprenticeship for a year or so, only being allowed on the foreshore in the company of an experienced club member. It may appear bureaucratic, but this can be a dangerous sport for the unwary. Quarry identification is also essential, and this can only be achieved under guidance from a wildfowler with years of experience behind him.

One of the chief hazards below the sea wall is mud. I discovered this the hard way when wildfowling in Chichester Harbour, an estuary notorious for its soft mud patches designed to trap the unwary. Eventually I learnt the art of mud walking, which involved taking short, quick steps with toes pointed down, but even so there was always the danger of being trapped up to one's waist in really cloying, deep mud. On one occasion I was present when a wildfowler had to be rescued by rope as he was inextricably stuck thirty yards (metres) from the shoreline and sinking. Mud pattens, resembling wooden tennis racquets and strapped to the feet, were once commonly used by wildfowlers but I have not seen them for many years.

Marsh craft and bird identification, a knowledge of tides, winds, currents and dangerous patches of mud, building a hide and returning safely, all come with experience, but once achieved the wildfowler can consider himself a member of an elite and very remarkable group of sportsmen.

As in all things, the written word is the basic key to knowledge, and the would-be wildfowler should arm himself with a modest library of books on the subject. One could not do better than to acquire *The Complete Wildfowler* by Stanley Duncan and Guy Thorne, *The Diaries of Colonel Peter Hawker*, *Wildfowlers and Poachers* by Arthur Patterson, *The Shore Shooter* by Richard Arnold, *Dark Estuary* by BB, *Wildfowling and Rough Shooting* by Noel M. Sedgwick and *The New Wildfowler*. There are, of course, dozens more books on the subject, but these few provide the background, the history and the essence of the sport.

6
Wild Duck Chase

In 1981 the Wildlife and Countryside Act was passed, and as a result, the species of duck available to the wildfowler or duck shooter was reduced to eight. The loss to the sportsman of sea duck such as scaup, long-tailed duck, common scoter and goldeneye was of little consequence, as these are no adornment on the table. Prior to the passing of the act, I shot a drake goldeneye and had it roasted. It was quite inedible and tasted, I recall, akin to boiled seaweed. The simple fact is that any duck, even wigeon or teal, which has been feeding on the foreshore rather than on sweet inland grasses, is likely to taste muddy. Normally, duck shot inland are delicious, and a plump mallard, shot over September stubble, gets a four-star rating in my culinary game book. Ladled with orange sauce and accompanied by a decent claret, it will provide a meal that will repay all the missed shots and frustrations of duck shooting.

Identifying Duck Species

So, which duck are on the shooter's menu? Mallard, teal, wigeon, pochard, gadwall, shoveller, pintail and tufted are all available to the wildfowler, though I would rate the top three as mallard, wigeon and teal. Each has its own charms, is good eating and, under most circumstances, provides thoroughly sporting shooting.

For the novice wildfowler or duck shooter, correct identification is essential. Each species has a distinctive flight pattern and call, readily identifying them to the experienced shot, even when they are seen as dark blurs at dusk or dawn. Wigeon, for example, are often found in large packs, and in the sunlight their white bellies gleam as they turn and swing, while the *wheeooing* call from the cock bird is distinctive and so evocative of the spirit of wildfowling. The male or cock birds (never drakes!) have a russet head with a yellow flash, grey upperparts, white secondary covert and pure white undercarriage, while the hens are brown with a green speculum on the wing. These handsome duck breed around and to the east of the Baltic, and arrive on our shores in the autumn in numbers that depend to some extent on the severity of the weather on the Continent.

Perhaps the most exciting, fast flying little duck is the teal; it is also delicious eating. One of the most common ducks in winter, they are abundant visitors to our shores from September to April, arriving from northern Europe. The little cock bird is singularly handsome, with his red head streaked with green, grey upperparts and yellow under-tail. At dusk a pack of teal, swishing across and into a flight pond, the cock birds uttering their thin '*kreek*' call, will have the wildfowler in a state of sheer excitement as he tries to snap shoot the whizzing black silhouettes. On the table, teal are unbeatable and a fat brace will provide a superb dining experience for one person.

Sometimes teal can be found in huge, weaving flocks, diving over the mudflats, rising, falling and twisting against the sky. At other times one may surprise a spring of teal, as they lift in panic from a drain or gutter, to offer the wildfowler a rising, and surprisingly difficult, shot.

The Mallard

The most familiar duck is the mallard, one readily recognized by shooters and the public alike, who are familiar with semi-tame park lake and river duck, and whose numbers are often augmented by wild duck. Semi-tame mallard have a tendency to produce some very odd colours, occasionally leading inexperienced duck shooters to imagine they have shot a rare or new species. All-black duck with white markings, pure white or buff-coloured birds occasionally mingle with wild mallard and can easily cause confusion. However, if the shooter is ever in doubt about the identification of a duck he has shot, then he should consult an expert. Don't pluck and eat the bird and then tell someone you think you may have shot an American green-winged teal! If you have any doubts about the identification of a shot bird, always ensure that it is examined by an expert.

Many of our winter population of mallard are migrants, but there is also a very substantial resident population, which is constantly being augmented by reared duck, released by wildfowling clubs and game and DIY shoots. I would, however, avoid any shoot that releases mallard which, even if they can be encouraged to fly, do so at roof-top height, circling round and round their pond to be slaughtered by unthinking so-called sportsmen. I have seen this happen time and again, even to the extent of dogs being sent into the water to try and make the duck fly. This type of reared duck shooting is an absolute disgrace. Fortunately such shoots are becoming increasingly rare, but have not yet been entirely eliminated.

Where to Find Sporting Duck Shooting

The finest reared duck shooting I have ever encountered takes place on a West Wales shoot, close to the coast and natural marshland. Duck are reared out on the marsh, and are fed by automatic feeders so that their contact with humans is kept to a bare minimum. In the shooting season they mingle with hundreds of wild duck and geese, and in terms of flying ability are indistinguishable from their wild brethren.

As a general rule wild duck tend to rest during the day and feed at night, so in theory, there are two main flights at dawn and dusk as the birds move to and from their feeding and resting grounds. However, to complicate the issue, one must take into account the tidal conditions and the weather, either or both of which can upset your calculations.

When the moon is half or full, wigeon are more likely to flight well after dusk, so it is worth examining the foreshore for likely flashes of water, noting any feathers or droppings to show they are in use. Provided one can organize a hide within shooting range and, most vital of all, there is sufficient filmy cloud illuminated by moonlit to enable you to see the black bottle shapes of duck silhouetted against it, then outstanding sport can be had. Such a combination of circumstances may occur only once in a season, but if the duck are really flighting, great sport can be had. However, a dozen wigeon is more than enough to make a reasonable bag, and it is always wise to depart while the duck are still coming in.

Stubbling Mallard

At the beginning of the season, in the early days of September, whilst the foreshore shooter may garner the occasional mallard, teal or early wigeon, if the inland duck shooter can still find any stubble left, using decoys, he may be able to enjoy some early sport with stubbling mallard. At this time of the year these duck are in outstanding condition and take some beating on the table. However, such stubble is becoming increasingly rare, for today, as the combine leaves the field, the plough is poised ready to enter.

Duck are wary and unlikely to feed close to hedges where a hide can be erected. Only surveillance at dawn and dusk will show where the birds are stubbling, while a sure give-away is droppings and loose feathers. The only answer may be a bale hide in the middle of the field. Don't forget, that as is the case with birds coming in to land, the duck will be heading upwind, so that any breeze needs to be blowing over your shoulder. Furthermore, being cautious and wary, the birds will tend to circle several times before risking landing. Don't be impatient and fire a long, risky shot, as you will probably miss and ruin the flight.

If possible, choose an evening when a strong wind is blowing, as the duck will then tend to come in to the decoys without hesitation, while shots will also be muffled. When the light has gone, and provided there is a sky against which you can still see the birds, you can then stand in the open and shoot. You will, of course, have a reliable gundog with you to retrieve each bird as it is shot. If you wait for the end of a flight before gathering the slain, you will invariably lose birds. Besides, any wounded bird must be immediately gathered and despatched.

Don't forget to pick up your empty cartridge cases, even if it means returning in daylight. The farmer will appreciate your consideration, and you will also want to drop him off a brace of duck.

The Natural Marsh

Some of my finest and most memorable flight shooting has been over a West Sussex marsh with a natural acre or so of reed-dappled water. No excavation was required, the flash was natural, and wild duck and snipe loved it. The only effort put in was to feed the water with tailings throughout the season. The corn was sprinkled, once or twice a week, along the margins of the water, and care was taken not to over-feed for the benefit of rats. The water was nowhere more than a couple of feet deep and only a few inches at its margin, making it ideal for dabbling duck. There were tufts of grass and reed where birds could rest and preen, while out of season the 200 acres of marshland and its drainage gutters always held some nesting duck.

Sadly, such productive sporting marshes are now few and far between, and even if found will command a serious amount of rent.

The Created or Converted Flight Pond

If you cannot find the natural thing, then a created or converted flight pond is the next best, and can, if used judiciously, provide outstanding shooting. You may have access to an old disused farm pond, a piece of soggy spring-fed ground or perhaps a stream which can be diverted – though always remember that you may need permission before making any drastic excavations that could alter the water table. Therefore consult not only the farmer, but also the local water board to ensure you are in the clear.

There are few places in the countryside to which duck cannot be attracted. There will usually be a local population on lakes, reservoirs or rivers, and an attractive, well fed pool will soon be patronized. Deep water is not a requirement for a flight pond. Mallard and teal are dabblers, not divers, and prefer shallow, soggy margins to a pond, and a depth of no more than two feet in the centre. When excavating a pool always leave an island in the centre where duck can loaf, secure from vulpine attack. One can also make securely anchored rafts on which the birds can preen and doze.

Given the choice I would always opt for a small pool rather than an extensive lake. A pond the size of two tennis courts is manageable, and if planted round with screenings of willow and alder against the prevailing wind, can offer shelter. Hides can also be constructed from willow plantings, each trained into a circle with a narrow entrance and seat. They should not, however, be placed by the water's edge, but should be set well back to ensure sporting shooting. You may also require two sets of hide to cater for differing wind situations. Again, remember that duck will circle time and again to satisfy themselves that all is well before turning in to the wind to land, providing, as they do so, killing shots.

Once permission has been granted to excavate a pond, a mechanical digger will quickly do the job. Don't design the pool to be a simple circle, but set in bays and one or two modest creeks where duck can shelter. You are the designer, and your decisions at this point will have a lasting effect, so think the project through with care and take advice. Remember that a small pond, provided it offers security and food, may more readily attract wild duck than a large, exposed and deep lake – although such lakes are often used by duck during the daylight hours when they can rest some distance from the shoreline. At dusk there will then be a general exodus to dine at smaller ponds which are being fed in the shallows.

Established ponds are frequently enclosed by trees, making it difficult for duck to drop in through a tangle of branches. Some clearance may be required, taking into account the prevailing wind, which will dictate the ducks' flight approach.

When to Shoot Duck

Flighting duck at dusk is no sinecure and the odds are in favour of the birds. The light will be failing and the birds, particularly teal, can slip into the water almost undetected. If possible try and face the west and the setting sun. This is essential on an evening when there is no cloud cover and the only light comes from the pallid western sky. Ears as well as eyes must be used if one has any hope of success, while an experienced gundog will also indicate the presence of incoming duck, long before you see them, by an upward head movement.

Calling duck at dusk.

The first indication of fowl may be the piping of a cock teal or the purring grunt of a mallard, then black bottle shapes whirr across the water, often landing with a splash before you have been able to make them out or swing the gun.

If you can see mallard circling, then hold your fire. A hasty shot at long range may ruin the flight for the entire evening and only result in a pricked bird; instead, be patient and let the duck come right in. As they prepare to land they are at their most vulnerable and can be cleanly killed. Teal may flick across the water like tiny black rockets, but such is their speed that they often elicit snap shooting at its best. It's an instant reaction, which eliminates any mental calculations about lead.

If you think you have hit a bird but it does not immediately drop, try and watch to see if it suddenly collapses or falls into cover. In the dark you may only hear a thud after a shot, but instantly send your dog to try and recover the bird. This is where an experienced gundog is absolutely essential. In fact, no one should pursue fowl, above or below the sea wall, without an efficient dog. My personal choice has always been labradors, particularly for the foreshore. Strong and tough with a thick double coat, they are made for the sport. My local wildfowling club will not allow any member on the foreshore unless accompanied by a dog that knows its business, or else in the company of a wildfowler with such an animal.

If there is a strong moon, half to full, duck may flight late, and provided there is a thin cloud cover, sufficient to enable you to see any birds, then it is worth waiting past normal flighting time if no duck have appeared. Always make a point of calling a halt to shooting while duck are still flighting in, so that latecomers will not be deterred and will assume that the pond is a safe refuge. The same approach applies to the shooting of a flight pond – basically it should be little and not too often: once a fortnight or once every three weeks may be more than enough. Constant shooting will soon deter wild duck, no matter how much the water is fed.

I am no fan of reared mallard released on a water in the expectation that they will attract wild duck. Mallard are notoriously aggressive, and far from drawing in wild birds, they are far more likely to repel them.

Sport Over Flooded Meadows

Apart from flight ponds, excellent sport can occasionally be had over flooded meadows when heavy winter rains drench the land. However, too much rain resulting in extensive flooding is not conducive to successful

Setting out decoys on flooded ground.

sport, as duck then tend to sit out in the safety of distant and unreachable flooding. However, if you have the good fortune to obtain permission to shoot over a moderate stretch of flooded water-meadow, then decoys will be essential. Obviously a hide of some sort will also be required. This may be a netting hide erected on poles, similar to a pigeon hide, or circumstances may dictate the use of natural cover such as a hedge, fallen tree, ditch or reeds. Gateways and barbed-wire fences also offer sites for netting hides. You will also need a seat of some sort, not to mention rations and a flask of coffee!

Don't set your raft of decoys too close to wherever you are hiding, and take into account the wind. Flights of duck will come over high, spot the decoys, circle and turn into the wind to land. If you are between the decoys and the approaching duck you should be able to have some outstanding sport.

Gusty, wild weather will be an advantage and tends to keep duck on the move. If you are lucky enough to have permission to shoot over flooded ground just inside a sea wall, rough weather may send teal and wigeon darting in from the sea to calmer waters and easy feeding.

However, when shooting flooded inland water, always be extremely cautious and use a wading pole, such as a tall thumbstick, if you have to negotiate the floods. Ditches and gutters will be hidden, and it is all too easy to plunge into a concealed hazard. Remember, too, that your dog (because you will have a gundog with you) must also be looked after and given a dry place in your hide. When shooting flooded meadows or similar situations, a competent dog is absolutely essential, and each duck should be retrieved as soon as it is shot. If the animal is light coloured or has patches of white, then it is worth considering a waterproof camouflage coat to break up its outline.

Don't forget, too, that if you anticipate shooting a reasonable bag of, say, a dozen or so duck then you will need either a substantial side-bag in which to carry them back, or at the very least a sack.

Sport on Land Intersected by Ditches

If you are fortunate enough to have access to marsh or pasture land intersected by ditches and gutters you may have some sport walking them up in the early part of the season when cover is still dense. Mallard and teal will resort to quiet patches of water, only rising at the last moment. If you are working a dog, make sure that it holds back and does not work the bankside cover too far ahead or duck will spring out of range. Duck may also shelter under the bank of a river, especially where it bends, so one needs to approach cautiously.

If you have a wounded duck in the water then it may prove too cunning for even the most experienced dog, and will almost certainly baffle a youngster as it will dive every time it seems within grasp. An older and wiser dog may manage to retrieve the bird, but if there is any doubt about the outcome, then bring your dog out of the water and shoot the bird when it surfaces.

Shooting Below the Sea Wall

The world below the sea wall is indeed a place of magic, of vaulting skies and vast horizon, but it is also a potentially highly dangerous scenario, one which can trap even the most experienced of wildfowlers. Potential hazards exist in sudden rolling fogs and mists, in swift incoming tides, in deep hazardous gutters and the ever-cloying mud. Obviously conditions vary enormously round the coastline, but one should never be over-confident or treat the marsh with anything other than caution and respect.

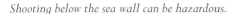
Shooting below the sea wall can be hazardous.

Mud and sand can shift from year to year so that a familiar and notorious patch may suddenly disappear, only to reappear nearby. Mud is so dangerous that not only can it trap the unwary, but it must, at all costs, be kept from entering the barrels of your gun. This is where a gun slip is essential when heading to and from your potential hide. Always carry a cartridge extractor, a sharp knife, and a workmanlike compass that you know how to use, and which can be strapped on your wrist. When you leave the sea wall and head out, take some readings so that, if fog does roll in, you will have a good idea of your bearings. If you intend to shoot on an estuary that you know can be dangerous, then a distress flare is a wise addition; the chances are that you will never need it, but one day you may bless having it aboard.

You will obviously have consulted a local tide-table, but do bear in mind the swift advance of an incoming tide. The water will race across the mud at an astonishing rate, filling the gutters and creeks that you previously negotiated when they were empty, but which have now become swirling rivers.

Safety Tips

If you are shooting on your own, then always let someone know when you are departing and when you expect to return. Also, make sure you have a mobile phone encased in a waterproof cover. This, in an emergency, could save your life.

7
The Sound of Geese

My goose-shooting exploits have been relatively few and far between, yet even today I can still recall with almost photographic clarity the occasion of each successful shot, the dry mouth-making moment when you knew, with certainty, that the geese were heading your way and would be in range. Even today, long past my modest goose-shooting exploits, the memories of outings to the Solway Firth, of the vast wavering army of geese pencilling across the waters and over the sea wall, remain pinpoint sharp. I can still feel the thumping recoil of the gun, and smell the evocative whiff of gunsmoke as a pinkfoot collapses and thuds as it hits the ground. That was a moment of glory – but there were all too many occasions when I missed, or there were calm, windless dawns when the great skeins came over two or three gunshots high.

Once a wildfowler is gripped by goose fever he will return, again and again, to pit himself against the grey hordes. He will know the splendour of the wild lands haunted by these magnificent birds, and feel himself to be so privileged to be able to engage in this meeting of man and bird.

Sadly, geese also seem to bring out the worst in so-called wildfowlers who, when the skeins of geese flight at dawn, appear quite incapable of restraint or of understanding range. I have stood on the Solway shore and watched as the geese have flighted over the sea wall, way, way out of shot, and stared in horror as gunners have pumped shot after shot into the air in the vague hope that an errant pellet might hit a bird in the head. Occasionally I have seen a goose pulled down from perhaps eighty or more yards (metres), a feat which only serves to encourage ignorant onlookers to try their luck.

There is little doubt that some high-flying geese are wounded by out-of-range shots, flying on to try and keep up with the skein and perhaps landing miles inland to become fox prey. They are tough, resilient birds, capable of flying for considerable distances even though carrying shot.

Identifying Geese

It is important to know which geese are now on the quarry list, and which are fully protected. In Britain, geese are divided into two categories: the black geese, which include brent, barnacle geese, Canadas and redbreasted geese – with the exception of Canadas, all these geese are fully protected; and the grey geese, which include greylags, pinkfeet, bean geese and white-fronts. These last are subdivided into Greenland, European and lesser white-fronts. Of the grey geese, pinkfeet and greylags are on the shooting list, while whitefronts may only be shot in England and Wales, though there is a moratorium on the species in Wales. The Greenland whitefront is protected in Scotland and Ireland, while the lesser whitefront and bean goose are fully protected.

So it is really only pinkfeet, greylags and Canadas that concern the wild-fowler and goose shooter. The grey geese are mainly to be found where there is stubble and on potato fields, where small frosted potatoes have been left to rot. They also favour pasture, winter wheat and early-showing corn in the late winter and early spring. Huge flocks of pinkfeet and greylags can cause severe damage to crops.

Whilst there is a small breeding population of greylags that tend to be mostly resident in their areas, the vast bulk of the population migrates to Britain from Iceland in the winter, with a few birds coming in from Scandi-navia. Indeed, the entire Icelandic population of greylags heads to Scotland, Northern Ireland and north-west England, only returning north in April to breed in their Icelandic fastness.

The Pinkfoot

The pinkfoot is the smallest of our grey geese and is readily distinguished not only by its pink bill and legs, but also by its brownish head and neck and its high-pitched *wink-wink-wink* call. Pinkfeet breed in Iceland and on the east coast of Greenland and Spitsbergen, but have never been known to breed in the British Isles.

Vast flocks of pinkfeet are found in winter on the eastern flanks of Scot-land, the Solway Firth, in the Morecambe Bay area and around the Wash on the east coast. The first birds arrive towards the end of August, the flocks steadily building up into the high thousands. A single roost may contain as many as 25,000 birds, providing a spectacular sight when they flight to the stubbles. When the pinkfeet first arrive on our shores they tend to concen-trate on spilt grain on barley stubbles, but as the plough moves in, then the flocks transfer their allegiance to potatoes and pasture.

Like greylags, pinkfeet tend to feed during the day, unless they are severely persecuted, flying at dawn to their feeding grounds, which may be many miles from their loch or their open sand sea roosts, and returning at dusk.

Pink feet dropping into a field.

The Whitefronted Goose

The third grey goose of these isles is the whitefronted goose, a species that is divided into two races: the European whitefront, which breeds in Siberia and Russia, and winters in England and South Wales; and the Greenland population, which only breeds in western Greenland, and winters in Ireland, west Scotland and Wales. Only the European whitefront can be shot in England, and there is currently a moratorium on it in Wales. The Greenland whitefront is now fully protected.

The whitefront is easily recognized by its black-barred underbelly, and it also has white feathers round the base of the upper mandible. In winter the birds tend to arrive from early October; the European race departs in March and April, while the Siberian population remains until late May.

Whitefronts will mingle with greylags and pinkfeet, but generally prefer to congregate in relatively small flocks or even pairs. In the air the whitefront is very agile; it also adopts the greylag's habit of half closing its wings to spiral down to a feeding area.

Behaviour

As far as the sportsman is concerned the grey geese all adopt a similar pattern of behaviour. During the night hours they will rest on inland lakes, lochs, reservoirs or floodwaters, or fly out to coastal sandbanks where they can roost undisturbed. The choice is to a certain extent dictated by pressure or otherwise of shooting.

Come the dawn the flocks will depart from their roost to their selected feeding grounds. In areas where shooting is a regular activity the flocks will swiftly assess potential danger, and in calm, placid weather conditions they will fly well out of range – it is only when a strong headwind, gale or fog greets the dawn that they are forced to fly lower. Fog tends to bewilder the birds, forcing them to meander as though lost and uncertain of their direction.

During a period of full moon the normal regular pattern of flighting may change as the geese may choose to feed at night, when they often tend to flight in small parties rather than huge skeins. Only a clear sky with no hint of cloud will tempt them to flight under the moon, and then only in the latter part of the shooting season when the daylight hours are reduced, food is in short supply and the birds choose to feed again through hunger.

Shooting Over Decoys

Geese can, of course, be shot inland on their feeding grounds, provided the wildfowler has permission from the farmer or landowner – and regrettably, restraint is sometimes cast aside by ignorant and greedy shooters. It is very easy to make a massive bag of geese over decoys, and in the past some selfish and greedy Guns, some of them foreign and under the charge of so-called professional guides, have slaughtered decoyed geese on an industrial scale.

There is absolutely no reason why geese should not be decoyed on their inland feeding grounds, provided restraint is exerted. For most sensible sportsmen two or three geese per Gun is more than sufficient, and a time limit on the outing should be enforced to enable the geese to recoup and return to feed undisturbed. If you are setting out decoys yourself, don't set them in regimented fashion directly into the wind, but try to make them look natural, with small groups and one or two outliers. You will need at least a dozen decoys for them to be really effective. Try to ensure your hide is downwind of the decoy set, and sited perhaps twenty or more yards to one side. Shooting geese under these circumstances is not too difficult and restraint must be exerted, so I repeat, do not shoot more than you need for personal use. These are magnificent birds and deserve to be treated with respect.

Setting out goose decoys.

In the past there have been some appalling displays of unsporting greed, but fortunately today BASC controls the professional goose guide scenario, and the days of grossly excessive bags are now at an end. If you engage the services of a professional guide for goose shooting then make certain that he has been approved by BASC.

Guns and Ammunition

What gun and ammunition should you use? The answer is a 12-bore with heavy shot, No. 3 or 1⅞oz of BB from a 3in chambered gun. A goose is a heavy, powerful bird, and whilst a first-class Shot may be able to pull down a pinkfoot with his normal game gun, the majority of us are not so gifted. The usual advice from successful goose Shots is to ignore the bird's body but to shoot instead at the head, treating it as though it were a teal or snipe. However, easier said than done in the excitement of the occasion! Furthermore, if the bird is flighting, rather than planing down into decoys, it will be flying much faster than appearances will lead you to believe. The advice to try and miss the bird in front is sound.

Remember, too, that you may be crouching in a ditch or in a creek on the mudflats, and will have to rise and mount your gun in one movement. It is essential to perfect good mounting if you are to have any success — and this applies to any form of live bird shooting. You may be unable to engage in ideal foot movement, so it is worth practising your gun mounting under difficult circumstances. It is also worth gaining some idea of the size of a goose in flight at known distances.

If you have to deal with a wounded goose, be cautious. You may, and should, have a good dog capable of retrieving a goose, but an injured greylag, even if it has a damaged wing and cannot fly, can prove a formidable adversary. If you approach a wounded bird yourself be prepared to shoot again, as it may still be capable of flying. I am no advocate of the head twirling method of trying to despatch an injured bird, but instead always carry a loaded priest. A sharp crack on the bird's skull will cause instant death.

A basic problem for the newcomer to geese is estimating range in relation to size. It is essential to be familiar with the appearance of a grey goose at thirty, forty and fifty yards (metres), and one simple way to achieve this is to create a life-size silhouette of a greylag or pinkfoot with wings spread, and then to study it at these ranges. It will at least provide some indication of size, though the appearance of a silhouette with a background may appear very different to the real thing at the same range with sky above it.

What of the big bores? I am no great fan of these heavy, cumbersome guns, and while I agree that an 8-bore or 4-bore can hurl an impressive amount of non-toxic shot into the air (remember the lead ban!), neither is capable of the versatility of a 12-bore magnum. Certainly a 4-bore will pull down a goose at sixty or more yards, but I have to confess a certain degree of bias against these massive guns.

There was an occasion many years ago when whitefronts were still legal quarry in southern Ireland, which caused me a certain degree of anguish. I was on a week's shooting holiday in the west, and although some duck, hares and snipe had been shot, no goose had crossed my path. Then, by chance, I came across a flock of around 200 roosting on the edge of a lough. I decided that, at dawn next morning, I would lie in ambush, taking advantage of a stone wall to approach them.

That evening I got into conversation with an elderly visiting wildfowler who kindly offered me the use of his double hammer 4-bore. It was a solid 16lb, but would, I fancied, wreak fearsome destruction on the geese. The next morning, with the monster gun cradled in my arms, I crouched below the wall listening to the whitefronts 200 yards in front. For two hours they remained by the lough's edge until abruptly, with high-pitched yelps, they lifted and flew straight at me! There was only one problem – they were too close! As they topped the wall I fired the right barrel into the mass of birds and nothing happened, except the flock lifted in clamorous alarm. However,

I did manage to drop one goose with the left barrel (the recoil from each was alarming), and later discovered that it had been hit by one pellet in the neck. The simple fact was that I was hampered by the heavy, slow-swinging gun, whereas with my magnum 12 I might have achieved a right and left!

Canada Geese

Canadas are the heavy bombers of the goose world. These familiar geese were first introduced to this country as an ornamental bird in the seventeenth century, and were initially kept on country estate lakes, though there is a record of Canadas being present in St James's Park in 1678. By the end of the eighteenth century these black geese were feral, and a century later breeding flocks were to be found throughout the land.

The population countrywide is now immense, with large flocks making use of lakes, reservoirs and ponds where they foul the water and banks with droppings. Being large and heavy, with a typical gander weighing up to 12lb (5.5kg) or more, they can under some circumstances present a hazard to aircraft. Numbers have grown to such an extent that under licence these geese can be shot year round.

A Canada goose retrieved.

As a sporting bird they lack something of the excitement of the grey geese, but nevertheless can offer some excellent shooting, and they soon learn to become extremely wary if they are harassed. In flight, whilst they may appear slow, even cumbersome, they are deceptive and fly just as swiftly as the grey geese. Heavy shot should always be used, and the secret of achieving a bird dead in the air is to swing through the head. In fact, imagine that the head is a teal and ignore the massive body.

Canadas in their native land are migratory, but in Britain this instinct has been largely eroded so that birds are resident, only flighting to and fro from water to grazing. There is, however, an exception to the non-migratory habit, with birds from Yorkshire and a few other areas flying north to the Beauly Firth in Inverness-shire to moult.

Their diet is largely grass, often causing considerable damage to farming interests and soiling the ground. However, in their favour a Canada is an excellent bird on the table, provided it is a youngster and not a grizzled old gander. Plucking the bird is an arduous task, but it is worth it in the long run as the skin crisps up and retains any fat covering the bird.

8

Woodcock, Snipe and Golden Plover

Within my lifetime this chapter would have included, in addition to woodcock, snipe and golden plover, five additional waders: curlew, redshank, bar-tailed godwit, whimbrel, grey plover and jack snipe. However, the Wildlife & Countryside Act 1981 removed these birds from the shooting list. On reflection it was perhaps inevitable, but at the time, those of us who regarded ourselves as primarily wildfowlers were dismayed to think that a brace of redshank or a curlew or two would no longer feature in the bag. All these waders were good fare, and on a day when the duck or geese chose not to co-operate, provided some compensation for the wildfowler's efforts. However, these waders will never return to the shooting list, and we are therefore left with snipe, woodcock and golden plover – though for some inexplicable reason jack snipe, which is proscribed in England and Wales, still features on the shooting list in Northern Ireland.

Leaving aside jack snipe, the three waders remaining on the shooting list are all basically found inland, though snipe and golden plover may often be encountered below the sea wall, while a solid, hard freeze inland may force even woodcock to the foreshore.

Snipe

Inland snipe are usually encountered in marshy fields, boggy patches, lakesides, water-meadows, salt marshes beside streams, in cattle-poached gateways and even in fields of roots, while in bitter weather they may be found in the most unlikely spots. Indeed, like a will o' the wisp, snipe may be chanced upon almost anywhere, countrywide.

A resident and a passage migrant, our winter visitors arrive from Scandinavia, Iceland, western Europe, the Baltic and parts of western Russia. In the UK the highest density of birds is found in the north, with numbers declining in the southern lowlands. The overall population is in slight decline, possibly

Removing the pin feather from woodcock's wing.

as a result of loss of habitat, but even so, the winter population of snipe is estimated at over a million birds.

These small waders have a deserved reputation for presenting an extremely tricky shot. One school of thought claims that they should always be walked upwind so they will rise into the wind and turn, so making for an easier shot, while an opposing school prefers to walk them downwind. Frankly I have never taken a great deal of notice of the pundits, and have invariably found that whichever way one approaches a 'snipey' patch of ground, the birds will rise with a rasping *scaaap scaaap* to twist and dart away with a zig-zag flight.

Some Guns choose to shoot at the bird as it rises, while others, myself included, prefer to wait until it is twenty-five or thirty yards away and has straightened in its flight. Whichever method you choose, it is very much instinctive snap shooting, and without question, an acquired skill. If I analyse a successful shot at walked-up snipe I can only say that I have no recollection of lead, only of shooting at the bird. Not very helpful, I know!

Snipe drives can occasionally be organized, with varying results. Several Guns can be posted on an anticipated flightline, while one or two helpers with dogs can slowly walk or zig-zag across water-meadows, marsh or root fields. Whilst snipe will usually fly straight once well up in the air, they demand skilled shooting to be brought to book, and like feathered darts, will speed over the Guns and demand ample lead and swing for any hope of success – and with a strong wind behind them they are virtually untouchable. The same applies at evening flight when, with a tearing rush of wings and a light plop, snipe will dart down to a marsh or shallow water, often landing close and unseen to the Gun waiting for duck to flight, and even when disturbed will still fly low against the darkening background.

In the past, some astonishing bags of snipe have been recorded. In 1897 the Duke of Westminster shot seventy-four snipe and his two guests a further fifty-four on a snipe bog near his home at Eaton, Cheshire, while a Mr Robert Fellowes from Norfolk once killed 123 snipe to his own gun in one day at Buckenham Ferry, Norfolk, in November 1860. However, the story that a sportsman killed 1,999 snipe to his own gun in a season and then shot himself under the mistaken impression that he was the 2,000th snipe is not true: he actually killed more than the coveted number, but then committed suicide with his own gun.

The jack or half snipe is smaller than the common snipe: this little wader sits close, rising only at the last minute to fly weakly for twenty or so yards before dropping into cover again. Readily distinguished by its size and also the fact that its beak is nearly an inch and a half shorter than that of the common snipe, this tiny bird is still, as previously mentioned, legal quarry in Northern Ireland but fully protected in the remainder of Britain. Why anyone would want to shoot it is beyond comprehension.

Woodcock

Beside me as I write is a superbly mounted woodcock, prepared by a skilled taxidermist. The plumage of this lovely bird is a blend of autumn tints, of rufous browns, of dark and lighter shades and a paler brown-barred breast, and its eye full black.

Although there is a resident breeding population of woodcock in these isles, numbers are supplemented in the late autumn and winter by migrants from Scandinavia, Russia and Germany landing on the east coast and then moving westwards, influenced by the weather. Largely dependent on earthworms, supplemented by insects, hard frosts and iron-hard ground forces them to seek milder, warmer ground where they can use their long, sensitive bills to probe for food. Bitter weather in the eastern regions of the country will usually result in an influx of woodcock to western regions, notably Wales and the West Country.

From March to July resident breeding woodcock engage in a flight at dusk known as 'roding', when the male bird flies on a regular path with slow wing

Labrador retrieving a woodcock.

beats and uttering a curious call, the intention being presumably to impress a female and mate with her. The nesting season is from mid-March to mid-April and the usual clutch is four eggs, laid in a small scrape lined with dead leaves. The eggs hatch after about three weeks' incubation, and the chicks are able to leave the nest at once.

For many years it was alleged that woodcock carried their young in flight, lifting them between their thighs to remove them a short distance from any potential danger. This phenomenon was hotly disputed, and indeed denied by many observant naturalists and countrymen. However, indisputable evidence has shown that chick carrying does in fact take place, and has also been seen in other waders.

This unmistakable bird is unpredictable and mysterious, and invariably causes a frisson of excitement when it rises in woodland to weave through the branches, often too low for a safe shot as it flies down the line of Guns. Indeed, at one time the bird had a certain reputation as a cause of accidents in the shooting field, such was the excitement it created when seen. The tale is doubtless apocryphal, but it was often related round the dinner tables that the appearance of a woodcock outside covert would cause Guns to fall flat in expectation of a low and dangerous shot!

Perhaps, too, the fact that the woodcock is the subject of the much sought-after right-and-left, making the fortunate sportsman eligible for the famous *Shooting Times* Woodcock Club, may add to its reputation for occasional chancey shots! Sadly, although I actually founded the Woodcock Club, I have never had a right-and-left at woodcock. The only occasion that I had a distinct chance was while shooting in Norfolk, when I killed the first bird, but then lowered my gun just as a second suddenly emerged – and although that one was also duly nailed, lowering the gun from one's shoulder precludes membership!

In cover such as woodland, a woodcock getting up at one's feet or flicking across a ride can be an exacting shot, demanding snap shooting coupled with a sense of safety where any other Guns or beaters are concerned; in the open, however, it can present a much easier shot, tending to fly in an almost owl-like manner, though often too low for a safe shot. If you are shooting in line on a driven day remember that beaters are in front and pickers-up behind, so only birds seen against the sky are legitimate shots.

If you are fortunate enough to shoot a woodcock, then be sure to remove the pin feathers for your hat. These are the small, stiff and pointed feathers, about an inch (2cm) long and found on the 'wrist joint' of the wing. These feathers were at one time greatly prized by painters of miniatures to pursue their delicate art, and even today there are one or two artists who still make practice with them.

The knowing Gun will also break the bird's legs and withdraw the sinews. Woodcock are highly prized on the table, but the entrails should not be drawn.

The Golden Plover

The last of the waders, the golden plover, provides superb sport and is also delicious eating. It takes its name from the fact that in summer plumage its upper parts are flecked with yellow and black, while its head and underparts are black. In winter the upper plumage still retains yellow spangles on a brown background, while the belly is now white. There is a resident UK breeding population, estimated today at around 23,000 pairs, while in winter numbers increase to 400,000 birds as migrants arrive from the moorlands and tundra of Northern Europe and Eastern Asia.

Our summer breeding population is centred on the southern uplands and Highlands of Scotland, the western isles, the Peak District, North Yorkshire, Wales and Devon. There is also a substantial over wintering population in the western regions of Ireland, as I know full well, having shot the birds on the banks of the Shannon.

Golden plover generally fly fairly low in large packs, and can be found on the shoreline as well as inland. These waders are extremely fast, with estimates of up to 60mph (100km/h) or more, and can easily baffle even the most experienced shot. If they are flying too high, or out of range, a shot fired in the air will often bring the flock diving towards the ground, occasionally to give a chance with the second barrel. This does actually work, as I have personally discovered. At dusk the birds, on evening flight, will hurtle towards the ground and then skim along at head height. The bird has a plaintive, mournful cry, and in past and more romantic days has been associated with lost souls.

I have been lucky enough in the past to have eaten lapwings and both grey and golden plovers. All are delicious on the table, provided they have been feeding inland and not on the foreshore – and, of course, only the golden plover is still legal fare. If you get the chance to shoot a brace or so, you will be fortunate; and carefully roasted, they will provide an outstanding dish.

9
The DIY and Rough Shoot

I have deliberately linked together these two branches of shooting as they are intricately entwined, to the extent that the one is simply an extended version of the other; and they have a great deal in common. Today the traditional rough shoot is far less common or to be found than it was fifty years ago. In those far-off days the term 'rough shoot' basically implied any form of shooting other than formal game shooting, pigeon shooting and wildfowling. Indeed, the name itself was really a misnomer, something akin to coarse fishing as opposed to game fishing.

The Rough Shoot

The rough shoot varies enormously depending on where it is, and was, to be found, because although in parts of lowland Britain it has, if not vanished, at least diminished – and in parts of Scotland and Wales, too – a varied bag can still be shot on a day's walkabout. The great joy of a day's rough shooting is the pleasure of being able to work one's dog for a variety of game, to take hard exercise, and to know that the outcome of the day's sport depends solely on you and your dog. There are still low-ground shoots in Scotland and the Western Isles that offer a wide variety of sport, and at the end of the day your side-bag may hold a brace of grouse, a woodcock, a duck or two, a snipe and a rabbit or hare. You will have tramped for miles over the roughest of ground, but will experience a feeling of immense satisfaction in the knowledge that you have truly earned every successful shot.

A good many years ago I and two companions rented a 400-acre (160ha) marshland shoot in West Sussex, bordered on one side by a tidal river. The rent was, I recall, £200 a year, and the sport was outstanding and of a character that can only seldom be found today. The land itself was networked with gutters, and had several acres of wet, reed-filled grounds, which in the winter always held snipe. There was a natural, shallow flight pond, thick hedges and banks from which the spaniels usually ejected a pheasant or two, while hares and rabbits abounded. But it was the evening flighting that offered the finest sport. Mallard and teal came in to feed on the barley tailings, there was an occasional wigeon, and on one memorable occasion a small skein of whitefronts dropped in, to lose one of their number.

This was rough shooting at its very best, and for my money, it beat driven pheasant shooting hands down. However, such sport is now rarely to be found, and even if it becomes available, demands a substantial rent.

In many ways, though, the rough shoot of former days has now mutated into the DIY shoot, the relatively new phenomenon that is rapidly changing the shooting scene. Its development stems from the concept, on certain rough shoots with the benefit of suitable ground, that sport might be improved by putting down some pheasants and perhaps duck. Such a move would obviously entail a certain expenditure, which could be offset by bringing in a few more Guns to share the costs. In a complete change of course, the shoot would be thinking in terms of release pens, perhaps even rearing their own birds. Cover crops would be required to hold birds – and suddenly a whole new shooting prospect was being born and expanded.

The Standard DIY Shoot

Today, the DIY shoot has settled down into a fairly standard pattern. The basic concept is to provide moderate driven shooting at a reasonable cost. In order to do so, the Guns in the shoot are expected to make a financial contribution, which will obviously vary according to the size and ambitions of the operation, and also to participate in the running of the shoot. Most DIY shoots take in around eighteen or twenty members, each of whom pays a subscription based on the size of the shoot and the number of birds put down. Furthermore, work parties will be organized throughout the close season to maintain release pens, or where it is required to build them, to clear rides, to undertake any work needed in woods, and to look after cover crops – in other words, all the work on a shoot that is normally the responsibility of a full-time paid gamekeeper.

Rearing Poults

Virtually every DIY shoot, whatever its size, will buy in poults. Rearing one's own birds requires an investment in brooder housing, heating equipment and also the knowledge and time to look after chicks. Poults bought from a reliable game farm pay hands down in terms of time and financial outlay. At the time of writing, eight-week-old pheasant poults cost in the region of £3.40 per bird. There will also, of course, be an outlay for food, beginning with starter pellets specially formulated for pheasants, and then moving on to wheat when the birds are getting ready to go to wood.

Blue plastic feeders with either trays or spirals are essential.

A new DIY shoot will initially have to invest in the materials to build at least one release pen, and this will involve wire netting, plastic netting, poles and shelters – these can be simply corrugated iron sheets set on short poles, but at an angle so that rain can run off. Feeders can be placed under the sheets and a receptacle placed at the lower end to catch rainwater. Anti-fox grills will also be required, with pop-holes to allow birds to come and go. In addition, an electric wire round the pen is essential to deter foxes.

Most DIY shoots, when they first get under way, are budget conscious as the initial start-up costs can be substantial. On my own very small shoot we bought twenty metal drums with removable lids, and punched two slits at the base of each, using a chisel, so that birds could peck at pellets and grain. These worked reasonably well, other than in torrential rain when water seeped in and clogged the feed holes with balled-up pellets. We also then invested in half-a-dozen large blue plastic drums specifically designed as feeders, which have proved highly successful. These feeders can often be found second-hand on the market. We have used both feeders with spirals and trays set beneath the drums, and have found the latter to be by far the best.

If there are deer on the shoot then it is essential to protect the feeders with a surround of wooden posts held together with wire. If such protection is neglected, deer will simply knock the bins over to try and get at the contents.

Organization and Running Costs

Every DIY shoot varies enormously in terms of what it can offer and how much individual Guns are expected to pay as an annual subscription. This may vary from around £500 to double or treble that amount, depending entirely on the outgoings and anticipated sport. However, when broken down into, say, eight days sport, this works out at a very reasonable sum per day.

To keep costs at this relatively modest level no paid beaters will be employed, and instead a shoot day will be run on a walk-and-stand basis, where all the members of the shoot will be divided into two teams, each under its captain, and they will take it in turns to beat and shoot. Occasionally some shoots are able to incorporate into the beating line wives, girlfriends, lovers and youngsters, but this often tends to be on a somewhat haphazard basis!

Pigeon shooting is often available on a DIY shoot.

There is another variation on the DIY shoot, though it is, I imagine, fairly rare. In my own case I pick up with my two labradors on a substantial driven shoot with around twenty-four paying Guns who each buy up to three days a season to form teams of eight on a day's sport. There is an honorary keeper who happens to live on the shoot and who receives a modest sum for his work; he is assisted by his wife and a friend. Around 2,000 birds are put down plus a couple of hundred partridges, and bags are usually in the region of forty to seventy birds, but all are brilliant high fliers from steep slopes.

What is so unusual about this shoot is that the team of beaters, who appear each season, work for nothing other than a brace of birds if available, a day's shooting at the end of the season with the Guns acting as beaters, and a slap-up dinner with everyone, Guns and beaters alike, taking part.

In addition to the sport it offers during the shooting season, the DIY shoot can often provide pigeon shooting when the season is over, depending on whether February roost shooting is available and also what crops the farmer grows. Where there is a great deal of rape and spring sowings, a team of Guns from the shoot who are able to provide crop protection on a regular basis can ensure that the farmer is only too happy to co-operate where the shoot is concerned. Normally he will be paid to sow game crops where they are required, provided he has land available, but there are some shoots where the farmer himself is an honorary member of the shoot and takes a deep interest in ensuring that it succeeds.

Sharing the Load

Unfortunately, some DIY shoots suffer 'hard-core workers syndrome': in other words, whenever a work party has to be organized it is always the same group of stalwarts who turn out and undertake all the hard work. This inevitably leads to dissension and can, in severe cases, cause the break-up of a shoot. One shoot with which I am familiar operates on the principle that at the end of the shooting season a work party must be available once a fortnight, and that every member of the shoot is expected to turn out unless they have a reasonable excuse. Any malingerers who persistently fail to support the shoot in this fashion simply do not have their subscription renewed. It seems to work, especially as the shoot has a waiting list for potential members.

One of the basic essentials of the DIY shoot is to have one or two members, preferably retired but active, who live nearby and are willing to take on the role of honorary keepers. Once the poults arrive in July or early August it is really essential to ensure that the release pen is visited daily to ensure that food hoppers are topped up, that fresh water is available and the electric wire surrounding the pen is working and has not been shorted out by, say, a falling branch.

It may also be necessary, regrettably, to remove the remains of any poults that have been killed by buzzards. These raptors have now spread throughout the country, and despite assertions that they only live on worms, slugs, baby rabbits and road-kill carrion, they are, in fact, an absolute menace in a release pen when poults are between the ages of seven and twelve or so weeks.

Pest Control

Pest control is essential on any shoot, DIY or otherwise, and this largely revolves around control of foxes, rats, grey squirrels, magpies, crows and stoats. A network of tunnel traps can take a steady toll of grey squirrels, rats and the occasional stoat, while Larsen cage traps holding a decoy live magpie can be extremely effective in controlling magpies, provided they are sited during the spring when these pest birds are seeking to hold territorial grounds and are then not prepared to tolerate what appears to be an intruder on their patch. However, if a pest control programme is to be undertaken on the DIY shoot it is a legal requirement that traps are visited every day – and this is where a retired local shoot member is so valuable.

Polecats

There is another ground predator that is beginning to appear on the scene: polecats are now spreading out from their former fastness in Wales, and appear to becoming entrenched across the border to such an extent that it is now believed the polecat population in England is larger than in the principality. In addition, polecat-ferret crosses are also appearing, doubtless the result of lost escaped ferrets. In my own part of the West Country these animals are now frequently encountered and often seen as road kill casualties. A keeper friend on a substantial driven shoot in Dorset now kills around a dozen of these polecat crosses each year.

Rats

Anti-coagulant poisons can be used against rats, especially where these pests are attracted to feeders. However, the poison must be laid under some form of cover so that it cannot be reached by any creature other than the target animal. Where rats are plentiful, piles of bait, which is already mixed with a cereal, should be laid in holes or runs and covered with tiles, bricks or corrugated iron. The poison takes several days to take effect as it works slowly, so baits need to be topped up as they are consumed.

Foxes

Fox control is, regrettably, essential as these animals can be highly destructive and are serious predators of game; they are top of the pest league on any shoot. I have to confess that I have a problem with over-zealous fox control as I hunted on horseback for decades and have always held a sneaking admiration for this handsome but crafty animal. Although foxes can be snared or driven to guns, today by far the most popular and effective method of control is lamping at night. This practice is highly effective in the hands of skilled rifle shots and today has, regrettably, become a sport in its own right.

I have not the slightest problem with shoots controlling foxes on their own patch, a necessary requirement since the hunting ban in 2004, but unfortunately a minor industry has grown up around this activity involving the production of specialist rifles such as the .17 HMR rimfire, night telescopes and lamping kits, and as a result, foxes are being shot on an unprecedented scale. Vixens feeding cubs are targeted, as too are cubs, and whilst I can understand and agree with reasonable control, this almost fanatical desire to kill every fox that can be found, spotlighted or called up, goes beyond reasonable sporting control, and, in my view, is totally unjustifiable. Our native fox is a handsome, intelligent animal, which has a place in the wildlife chain and does not deserve to be slaughtered on such a scale.

There was a time when it was common practice to shoot at a fox that appeared on a driven shoot day. However, Guns would, of course, only be armed with light shot, which is totally unsuitable to kill an animal weighing anything from 14 to 20lb (6 to 9kg) and heavier, unless it is very close. The result, too often, was an injured fox escaping, to later die of its wounds. There was also the safety factor to consider, as an excitable Gun might be tempted to take a risky shot as a fox crossed the shooting line. However, today all ground game, including rabbits and hares, are banned on driven days, largely because of the safety factor.

Magpies and Crows

Every effort should be made to control and, ideally, eliminate magpies and crows, and this is especially the case if you are fortunate enough to have any wild pheasants or partridges on your ground. These corvids will assiduously quarter the ground for any sign of nests, and if they discover any, will take every egg. Crows can be destroyed in the spring when they are nesting, though it can be incredibly frustrating to see the hen bird slip off the nest as you approach, and always in a manner to ensure you cannot get a shot. However, if there are two of you and you approach from different sides, the bird may well be caught out. A charge of heavy shot, such as BB or No. 3, into the nest should wreak havoc and destroy any eggs.

However, today the best defence, certainly against magpies and crows, is the Larsen trap. It was designed by a Danish gamekeeper in the 1950s, and since its introduction it has revolutionized the control of these two species on shoots. The trap is designed to catch corvids alive, using a decoy bird, so it is divided into three compartments, with half the trap used to hold the decoy bird, and the other half divided into two catching compartments with spring-loaded trap doors. It is highly effective and is based on the urge of both magpies and crows to evict any apparent intruder into their territory during the spring nesting season. The key to success is to keep moving the trap to fresh sites once a capture has been made.

For many newcomers to the Larsen trap, the initial problem is catching the first decoy bird. One answer is to contact a local gamekeeper who is also using Larsen traps, and negotiate a live magpie or crow that he has caught, but failing this the trap can be baited with a few eggs and sited under a bush or foliage close to a spot favoured by corvids. Broken egg shells can be scattered round the trap to give the impression that this is a predated nest, which must be taken advantage of. The trap must be checked at least once a day, preferably twice, and if on the first visit a bird has been caught, it can be left till late in the day in the hope that its mate will also be trapped. A trapped bird must be humanely destroyed, and a quick, hard blow to the head will suffice.

The live decoy bird must be looked after humanely. The decoy compartment must have a cover to protect the bird from rain and sun, while two perches should be included as these will inspire the bird to hop from one to the other, the movement helping to ensure that it is spotted by a potential target bird. Fresh water contained in water bottles attached to a trap side and food in the form of tinned dog or cat food can be used, or a split open rabbit, though this will attract flies in warm weather. Food must be replaced daily, and some should also be placed in the catching compartments for any captive birds. The welfare of your decoy is in your best interests, as a healthy, vigorous bird will call and attract target birds.

The siting of a Larsen trap is critical, not only from the point of view of catching corvids, but also to ensure that it is not spotted by the public and vandalized. The trap does not have to be placed in the open, but is in fact likely to be more effective under cover in a wood or copse. The calling decoy will attract the attention of any magpies or crows that have a territorial interest in the area.

The Feral Cat or Hunting Cat

Another predator that can cause mischief is the feral cat or hunting cat. These animals can be inveterate killers, not just of mice and similar 'small deer', but they will readily kill poults if they can gain access to them. The vast cat population in Britain takes a massive toll of wildlife, though organizations such as the RSPB prefer not to draw attention to the subject for fear of upsetting all those probably more elderly people who contribute to their funds, and who fondly believe that their 'fireside' moggy would never so much as look at a bird!

Setting Up the DIY Shoot

What is involved in the establishment of a DIY shoot? It is very unlikely that you and your fellow Guns will try to rear your own birds using broodies. It is a charming thought, and pheasants or partridges reared under broodies are undoubtedly hardy and more worldly wise than their incubated cousins. However, whilst in the years up to the last war, and even for a few years

---

Animal Rights Activists

Whilst poaching for gamebirds no longer takes place on the scale it once did, largely because the market is to some extent flooded with game and there is no, or little, profit to be made from an assault on a shoot, in this age of political correctness, animal rights activists can be a menace. Few have any knowledge of the countryside, its wildlife or how it is managed, and have been known to destroy release pens and game-rearing equipment. This type of activity sometimes results through frustration at failing to interfere with a hunt going about its lawful business, and is more a case of petty, mindless spite than a targeted assault.

If you are starting a DIY shoot, or have one under way, it is wise to keep the details to yourself and shoot members only, rather than disclose any information in the local hostelry. Walls have ears and information may be picked up by the 'wrong' people. If you are unfortunate enough to be paid a visit by antis on a shoot day, it is essential that every gun is unloaded and sleeved. Confrontation is pointless, and the simple answer is to call the police immediately.

thereafter, all game shoots reared their birds using broodies on the open field, this time-consuming method has long gone by the board, replaced by artificial but highly successful rearing systems. Besides, it is now almost impossible to find broodies on anything other than a tiny scale.

The game farm has long been the prime source of game birds and mallard, and while extensive game farms produce birds on a massive scale to supply driven shoots countrywide, there are also smaller game farms which can readily supply poults and duck on a scale to suit the DIY shoot.

The Release Pen

Assuming a group of potential Guns has acquired a tenancy agreement over a block of land, then one, or even two, release pens will be required, depending on the number of birds to be released. It is generally accepted that a pen enclosing an acre of ground should hold no more than 300 birds. If too many poults are introduced disease and feather-pecking may break out, while in addition the wood's plant life will also suffer severe damage. The pen itself should ideally be sited in the centre of the shoot in a sheltered, warm deciduous wood. It is pointless to establish a pen in the vicinity of a shoot boundary,

A DIY shoot release pen.

as birds will inevitably stray over the border for the benefit of a neighbouring shoot. Avoid at all costs conifer woods, which will invariably preclude any sunlight and as a result have a barren, empty ground base.

If, having chosen a site for the pen, you discover that it is heavily shaded by overhanging branches, then fell some trees to let in sun and light, leaving the dropped trees where they are to provide cover, shelter and the first stages in roosting for the birds. However, before dropping any trees check with the shoot owner (and the landower, if this is not the same person) that this is acceptable. Ideally the pen should contain an area open to the light and sun, another area holding cover for protection against bad weather, and a third patch with tall, well branched trees to encourage roosting off the ground as the birds mature.

In siting your pen, remember that you will require easy access for feeding and topping up water. You do not want to be struggling through undergrowth to get to the pen, so a nearby ride that will take a vehicle is essential.

Construction of a release pen will involve the following items: tanalized posts some eight feet (two metres) high, wire netting for the base of the pen, and either wire or plastic netting (I favour the latter) for the top. There will have to be an entry gate, which will require timber, hinges and latches, re-entry 'pop-holes' with anti-fox grilles and wire wings to guide the birds, two-strand electric wire and a 12-volt car battery, and some means of supplying water. You will also, of course, require a supply of nails and tools.

If there is no immediate access to water then, as I know all too well on my own shoot, the only answer is a supply of plastic water carriers (we use six in our 300-bird pen, topping up the supply on a regular basis). A constant supply of fresh water is as essential as food, otherwise birds will stray in search of it.

The release pen must be constructed with care and forethought. I have seen too many pens with weakened poles, flopping wire, and holes where a stoat, mink or fox cub could enter.

Before constructing the pen, the site must be marked out and a fencing line cleared. A track at least three feet (one metre) wide to incorporate the pop-holes and their wings will need to be cut, so that the pen can be walked round and inspected and any overhanging branches cut back. Whilst some authorities advocate a central ride cut through the pen where feeders can be placed, I have found that feeders dotted round the principal open area in the pen, supported by at least two shelters that will also hold feeders, work very well.

The fence posts should be at least six feet (two metres) high from the ground, and some ten or twelve feet (three or four metres) apart. Two strands of taut wire, one at the top of the poles and the other half way up, will act as supports for the wire netting. Wire can be used for both top and bottom, but I have found that plastic netting works very well for the top position and can be secured to the straining wire with pig rings. The bottom foot of the wire netting is bent outwards and secured firmly to the ground with long metal staples. It is absolutely essential that this section of the wire is flat to the ground and cannot be lifted by a predator such as a stoat, rat or fox, even though the electric wire is working as a deterrent.

For water containers I have used a combination of large plastic bottles cut in half, and circular flat trays with a slight rim. It is surprising just how much water poults will consume, and certainly for the first few weeks the containers will need to be topped up daily, as too will the feeders. In the pen we have used tin drums with two slits punched in the base using a chisel and hammer, and these are placed under shelters. These drums have lids and can be quickly refilled. More elaborate (and costly!) feeders can be acquired, but ours work perfectly well.

Once you have an arrival date for your poults from the game farm, switch on the electric wires a few days before arrival and make sure you are already stocked up with growers' pellets. The birds will be about seven or eight weeks old when they arrive, and will quickly settle down once they have found the feeders.

Managing the Release Pen

The pen must be visited daily to top up feed and water and to check that no unwelcome visitors have got in. We have found that, whilst we have had no trouble from foxes when the birds are penned, the same cannot be said for buzzards. These raptors are fully protected by law and are now widespread, and are a menace until poults are about ten to twelve weeks old. They will perch on nearby trees and from there drop on the young birds, killing and eating them in the pen. A six-inch (15cm) nail driven into the top of each release-pen pole will at least deter the predators from perching on these, while you can also hang up white feed bags and twirling CD discs – and some keepers swear by a radio tuned to Radio 1! We tried this one year but it seemed to make little difference, and we quite quickly gave up as a result of exhausted batteries and a soaking by rain.

You can attempt to feed buzzards away from the pen with shot rabbits, slit open, but while this may work for a few days, there is the added risk of attracting foxes, magpies and crows to the complementary feast. In theory, you can apply to Natural England for a licence to remove buzzard nests once the nesting season is over, or even, as a last resort, to kill the birds, but any such licence issued will immediately attract the attention of the RSPB who will strongly oppose any suggestion of buzzards being targeted – despite the

Buzzards, whilst fully protected, can be a menace when poults are first released.

fact that they are happy to kill crows, magpies, gulls, foxes and deer on their own reserves. It is a no-win situation that shoots are obliged to put up with.

When the poults are first introduced to the pen, the pop-holes should be closed for three or four days using rolled-up newspaper. Once opened, the birds will very gradually begin to trickle out and back in again. Once they are about ten weeks old you should start to supplement their feed with wheat until at three months old they have been weaned on to this grain and are off pellets completely. At this age, too, the birds will be feathering up, tails will be growing and the cocks beginning to colour up. They will be spreading out from the pen during the day, and it is now essential to ensure you have feeders in the vicinity of the pen. These should be the large blue plastic containers on three legs with feed trays at their base. Each will hold a considerable amount of wheat and will only have to be refilled on a weekly or even longer basis. Scatter straw round the feeders and sprinkle some grain in it, as the birds will love scratching for it.

Basically, you will need to site feeders strategically in nearby woods or copses so that as the pheasants move out in search of food, they are still con-tained within the shoot boundaries and can be driven back, on shoot days, towards the pen. Every shoot is different, as too are the drives, but the basic principle is not to drive birds towards or over the boundaries as they are then likely to be lost, especially if you have neighbouring shoots.

On this subject, good relations between neighbouring shoots are essential. Nothing is worse than a boundary 'war', with one shoot placing feeders or planting cover crops with the intention of luring the other shoot's birds over the border. Every attempt should be made to ensure that neighbouring shoots work together for their mutual benefit.

As a rule of thumb, pheasants should not be shot before they are at least twenty weeks old, and preferably two or three weeks older than that. Today, most driven and DIY shoots get under way around the middle to end of October, with perhaps a walked-up day round the boundaries a week before that. One can, therefore, work backwards from the first shoot date to the arrival date for the poults, which of course will already be seven or eight weeks old.

Disease: Avoidance and Management

Apart from the constant threat from predators during the release-pen and immediate post-pen stages of rearing, disease is another hazard which can all too easily wreck all the hard work that goes into rearing and releasing pheasants. Today, a significant disease which has resulted in considerable losses is Hexamita, or Hex, as it is commonly known. Transmitted through faecal contamination, it is a major cause of death during rearing and immediate post-release. The symptoms are depression, diarrhoea and severe weight loss. Research into the disease is still under way, but it appears possible that the development of a glucose and electrolyte solution for oral administration may combat it.

Another problem disease is Mycroplasmosis, or, as it is more familiarly known, 'bulgy eye'. This disease has been recognized since the 1950s, and though most often seen in adults, there is also a high death rate amongst seven- to fourteen-week-old poults. The symptoms are sneezing, conjunctivitis, watery eyes, nasal discharge, reluctance to move and slow growth. The disease can be caused through infected litter and air droplets, and the problem is that while infected adults may recover, they will still carry the disease, thus infecting the entire flock. Antibiotics can control the problem but won't eradicate the disease.

A third disease to watch out for is gapes. This respiratory problem is caused by the gapeworm, sometimes known as the red worm or forked worm. It is a parasitic nematode worm infecting the trachea by clogging the airway and causing the bird to gape or gasp for air, making a hissing sound as it does so. Young birds infected with gapeworm usually die as they stop drinking and become anorexic; adults are usually less severely affected. The drug Invermectin is used to control infection, while Thiabendazole is an effective treatment in feed.

If you suspect an outbreak of any of the above diseases, or some other associated problem, the immediate answer is to have one or two birds under suspicion checked by a vet conversant with gamebird problems, and advice can be obtained through the good services of the National Gamekeepers' Organization. Any delay or hesitation could cost a small shoot an entire season's sport.

However, sensible precautions can reduce the threat of disease to a minimum. If you have a release pen that cannot be moved to another site, and this is often the case with the majority of small DIY shoots, simple precautions will usually keep your birds relatively free from disease. It is a waste of time spreading lime on the pen ground unless you have a soil that is so alkaline that nothing will grow on it. Diseases love a soil with a neutral ph, so spreading lime in the pen will, in the majority of cases, actually improve the conditions for disease pathogens.

I know a professional gamekeeper, some of whose release pens are twenty or more years old and have remained on the same site for that period, yet he has had no major disease problems. The most important factor is to make sure that each batch of poults is disease free when they arrive. In addition, washing and disinfecting drinkers and feeders should keep disease to a minimum, but use a 'hatchery' standard disinfectant when washing, as a normal 'farm' standard disinfectant will not destroy all the bugs.

If you are sufficiently sophisticated to have installed an automated drinking system in the pen, as opposed to hand-filled drinkers, use an item called 'Aqua 6' in the header tank. This will clean the pipes, prevent a build-up of bacteria and sanitize the water at the same time.

Every year, birds should be treated against gape and other worms by the addition of a control agent such as Flubenvet to their feed. The worm cycle is simple: eggs will be picked up in the soil, in faeces or earthworms, and in a few hours will have hatched as larvae in the lungs. A week later the worms will be in the windpipe, causing the bird to gasp for air. Three weeks later eggs produced by the worms will be shed by the bird to contaminate the soil and continue the cycle.

Cleanliness and simple precautions around the release pen, feeders and drinkers should ensure peace of mind and disease-free poults.

Game-Cover Crops

Game-cover crops are an essential part of any driven game shoot. They provide cover and food for both pheasants and partridges, and certain crops have the additional benefit of providing winter feed for a wide variety of wild birds. Where the crops are sited is critical as they will be used to contain birds and ensure that, when driven, they head into, not out of, the shoot.

Co-operation with the farmer is, of course, essential as he will be responsible for drilling crops and will also be in a position to know the soil conditions and which cover crops are most likely to prove successful. In addition, he may also be involved with the Single Farm Payment Scheme, which encourages him to re-plant hedges and manage field margins to encourage insects and wildlife. If this is the case it will also be a bonus for gamebirds.

The choice of game-cover crops can be dictated by the soil type, and before ordering any seed it may well be worthwhile bringing in a game-food expert to analyse the soil and offer advice. The most common and popular game-cover crop is undoubtedly maize. It provides adequate cover and a source of good quality food, and should last well into January. It can also be mixed with kale, a crop that will normally last for two years.

Other choices include quinoa, which produces a high protein food but must be well fertilized, millet, sorghum, artichokes, canary grass, buckwheat, sunflowers and linseed. Another valuable plant is triticale, a rye/wheat hybrid that seeds throughout the winter, and which has a tolerance of poor soil. Mixes of various plants can also be obtained. Much depends on the weather, timing and the farmer, but it is advisable to take the advice of a local game-cover company who will offer specialist advice.

Partridges

Now what about partridges? Such has been the decline of the native grey partridge over the past half century as a result of loss of insect life due to pesticides and the grubbing up of hedgerows, that today one automatically thinks in terms of red-legged partridges. Indeed, shoots are exhorted not to shoot greys, which are struggling to make something of a tentative comeback, particularly where shoots and farms make every effort to provide an ideal environment.

The red-legged partridge, or French partridge, is native to the Mediterranean, the first birds being imported into East Anglia in about 1770 where they soon became established. However, it took many decades before the bird spread across much of the remainder of the country. Less dependent on insect life, chicks will consume seeds and vegetable matter, while the redleg hen also lays a double clutch of eggs, one of which is incubated by the cock bird.

In 1963 several shoots and game farmers realized the advantages that lay with the redleg, and in the late 1960s game farmers also discovered that the closely related chukar partridge was highly prolific in captivity: these birds became very popular on low-ground shoots. However, it was soon discovered that the chukar would crossbreed with pure wild redlegs, and in hybridizing, introduced a serious problem: whilst chukars bred well in captivity, this attribute did not apply to the wild. Hybridization therefore threatened the purity of redlegs, and as a result the releasing of chukar and chukar/redleg hybrids was prohibited in 1992.

So should the relatively small DIY shoot give any thought to releasing redlegs? My advice would be a firm negative in most cases. Time and again I have encountered shoots that have experimented with redlegs, putting down perhaps 100 or 150, but often the returns have seldom reached double figures. However, on a large acreage and where the terrain is suitable, redlegs can provide brilliant sport. Some of the shallow valleys and banks in Wiltshire, particularly on Salisbury Plain and the surrounding chalk downlands, can offer outstanding shooting, with the birds driven from cover crops planted out of sight on the summit of the downs. I have seen huge packs of redlegs crossing the line of Guns in September and October, and the same applies to some of the West Country shoots in Somerset, Devon and Cornwall. But these are large, professionally organized shoots, often operating on a commercial basis.

As previously noted, the West Dorset shoot of 1,000 acres where I pick up releases around 2,000 pheasants and 150 redlegs. The young birds are initially kept in their own pens which are themselves sited in the pheasant release-pens and released when the pheasants begin to roam outside the pens. It seems to work, though the number of partridges shot in a season is seldom more than a score or so. They do, however, add an extra dimension to the day and the Guns always seem to appreciate a few partridges whirling across the line.

Bluntly, I believe that a relatively new DIY shoot is best occupied concentrating on rearing and releasing pheasants in its formative years. Once the shoot has settled into a pattern, then perhaps, if the ground is suitable, thought can be given to adding redlegs to the mix.

In Summary

Today, the DIY shoot is rapidly expanding as groups of sportsmen choose to create their own shoots. The scale and size of the shoot is entirely dependent on land available and what the team of Guns is prepared to invest in the venture, both in terms of money and time, but the end result can be immensely satisfying, both from the point of view of the sport itself, and also the acquisition of intimate knowledge about the countryside and its wildlife.

10
Driven Shooting

The formal driven shoot still remains at the centre, the heart, of live shooting and has been a cornerstone of the sport since the middle years of the nineteenth century with the introduction of the first breech-loading shotguns. Prior to this major innovation in the world of firearms, sporting shooting had been to some extent constricted by virtue of the fact that guns, whether flintlock or percussion, had still to be loaded from the muzzle, a lengthy procedure that could not be adapted to the driven sport.

Developments in Sporting Firearms

Loading a flintlock demanded time and care. A charge of powder had to be poured down the barrel from a flask, followed by a wad using a ramrod, then a measure of shot from another flask, the entire charge being held in place by a further thin wad. There was, in addition, the risk of rain or damp causing a misfire. The same loading procedure had to take place with a percussion gun, including placing caps on the nipples. Neither the earlier flintlock nor the latter percussion system could be satisfactorily adapted to driven shooting, and it was not until the 1850s and 1860s when the first breech-loading systems began to appear that driven shooting really got under way.

Those early breech-loaders were, initially, complicated and even crude. Barrels slid forwards or sideways, and the first cartridges depended on the needle or pinfire system. It was not until 1861 that a central fire cartridge was introduced by a Mr Daw: he was the sole exhibitor of central-fire guns and cartridges at the International Exhibition of 1862.

The gun-making world applied for patents, and in a frenzy of invention designed a variety of central-fire hammerguns so that by the 1870s the breech-loading gun in various guises reigned supreme. However, this reign shortly came to a swift end with the advent of the hammerless gun, brought to perfection by the Anson and Deeley gun, which was cocked by the barrels. Improvements included the ejector system and single triggers, so that by the end of the nineteenth century the hammerless shotgun, in side-lock and box-lock form, had reached near perfection.

Evolution of the *Battue*

These developments in sporting firearms were paralleled by the switch from walked-up shooting to the *battue*, the innovation from the Continent which completely transformed the shooting scene in Britain. Now, instead of tramping all day in the hope of a shot at a departing partridge or pheasant, pausing after each shot to undertake the lengthy business of reloading, the sportsman could stand and have birds driven over him by a team of beaters.

It was, however, very much a sport pursued by the higher echelons of society and the great county families, led by royalty. Shooting house parties became an established way of life in the season, with almost semi-professional shooting men moving from one estate to another – provided, of course, that their skill at dealing with vast numbers of driven pheasants and partridges was beyond criticism. Such renowned shots as The Hon. Harry Stonor, Lord Herbert Vane-Tempest, Lord de Grey, King George V, Lord Walsingham, and Prince Victor Duleep Singh, to name but a handful, moved from one estate to another, feted by their owners and leaving in their wakes thousands upon thousands of birds slain with a degree of elegant nonchalance, while lesser mortals could only look on with subservient awe.

The numbers were astonishing. The Maharajah Duleep Singh killed 780 partridges in one day to his own gun for 1,000 cartridges, though it has to be admitted that he kept on having the unfortunate birds driven over him repeatedly, while Lord de Grey shot over 100 partridges in one drive. The abundance of grey partridges in those days was phenomenal: in 1887, 4,076 partridges were killed in four consecutive days by seven Guns at The Grange, an estate in Hampshire. Perhaps the most remarkable feat was achieved by Lord Walsingham, who, on 30 August 1888, shot to his own gun 1,070 grouse on Blubberhouses Moor in Yorkshire. He began at 5.12am with alternate drives, up- and downwind, and then walked home at 7.30pm. He fired black powder cartridges all day, suffered neither headache nor bruising, and spent the rest of the evening playing cards!

It was the so-called Golden Age of driven shooting, a brief interval of around forty years before all the cards were to tumble down with the advent of the Great War in 1914. The days of unfettered shooting, vast bags and lavish house parties were now history. Driven shooting would revive in the 1920s and 1930s but on a more modest and far less ostentatious scale.

The Post-War Period

After World War II, with many estates reduced and broken up, experienced gamekeepers in short supply, and a realization amongst all aspects of society that getting Britain back on its feet was a priority, driven shooting was placed on the back burner. However, before too long open rearing fields, with their long rows of broody hens mothering clutches of eggs, once again came into operation, and albeit on a greatly reduced scale, the driven shoot once again began to play a commanding role in the shooting scene.

Private shoots still provided the backbone of the sport, but the syndicate was soon to appear, and before too long would dominate the driven shooting world. By 1958, the year of the very first CLA Game Fair, held at Hall Farm, Stetchworth, Cambridgeshire, the open field rearing system was on its last legs. Most keepers were still employing broody hens in conjunction with the moveable pen, but a rearing exhibit at the Fair introduced new methods of artificial incubation using calor gas, electricity or paraffin for heating. The very latest rearing techniques, developed by the then Game Research Station, were on display and were soon to transform the shooting panorama. Rearing would now take on a completely different aspect and would also extend to the game-farming scenario. The entire driven shooting scene was on the cusp of a change that would have a major impact on its future.

This transformation in rearing methods was to bring about a significant alteration to the driven shooting scene itself. Private shoots still remained at the heart of the sport, but the syndicate shoots were now snapping at their heels. The system was simple: a group of eight or nine Guns would each pay an annual subscription, its size based on the number of birds to be put down, the cost of renting land, and the provision of one or more gamekeepers. This system proved extremely popular, and as a result, the syndicate shoot flourished – and today still has a significant role to play in the world of driven shooting.

The Commercial Shoot

It would not be long, however, before the commercial shoot appeared on the scene. Large shoots and estates realized that there was a viable market for days of sport sold on a commercial basis, and to a large extent this system, which depended on selling individual days of driven shooting, quickly became established. Clients could now choose the number of days they wished to shoot, the size of the bags, and how much they were prepared to pay.

However, the system drew down upon itself a degree of censure, partially justified, in the 1980s and 1990s when institutions such as banks bought shooting days for clients and staff quite simply as 'jolly days out', regardless of the ability, skill or understanding of the countryside by those who took part. I can recall instances where participants who had never handled a gun before were given a clay pigeon shooting lesson in the morning, and then, after a substantial lunch, let loose in the afternoon on partridges or pheasants, with dire and dangerous results.

At this time the commercial shoot was its own worst enemy, and while many were run on well managed and responsible lines, there were others that chose to ignore sporting values, and instead put down vast numbers of birds, killed excessive bags, and even released penned birds on the day of a shoot. There were reports of birds being buried at the end of a day's so-called sport, and action had to be taken to recover the good name of shooting. The outcome was the publication of *The Code of Good Shooting Practice*, a document produced by a consortium of organizations and associations all concerned with the welfare and advancement of shooting, and which laid down the requirements and practice necessary to produce a reasonable and legitimate day's driven shooting.

The document clearly spelt out the basic requirements expected of a private, syndicate or commercial shoot, to include respect for quarry, the retrieval of all shot birds, and which, in turn, must be used as game food, while there were also requirements on shoot managers to enhance wildlife conservation and the countryside. Guidelines were also issued on the sustainable releasing of gamebirds, and emphasis was placed on a ban to replace birds that had been already shot in a season.

Commercial shoots play an important role in the shooting scene nowadays, catering in particular for visitors from overseas, and also for those who prefer not to belong to a syndicate, but would rather buy days at a variety of locations countrywide, each offering a different slant on the driven shooting scene. It is true that there has been some criticism of the size of bags at some locations, but it can also be argued that it is totally irrelevant whether a team of Guns shoots 150 birds or 650; it is only in the public perception that some disquiet may be seen.

Today it is generally accepted that 100 to 200 birds shot in one day is a reasonable and acceptable bag, one which will have offered all the Guns taking part ample sport. Views on this may differ, and there are those who would prefer to shoot a considerably larger bag. In favour of moderate bags, though, is the perception that at least those taking part will be able to recall memorable shots, whereas a day of non-stop action is likely to be a blur of shots taken and shots missed.

For the tyro the driven day can be something of an ordeal: the right clothing, the right gun and cartridges, tipping and an understanding of the long-established traditions – all the elements that are second nature to the old hand can be a source of extreme anxiety to the novice. The answer is familiarization before ever attending that first shoot. If you know someone who regularly shoots on driven days, then wheedle your way into his favour and attend a shoot or two as an observer, or if you want to be involved for a season, volunteer as a beater on a local shoot. You will be at the wrong end of the action, but will at least begin to understand how a shooting day works.

As I have emphasized again and again, before you even come to contemplate buying a day's shooting or joining a syndicate or DIY shoot, take a series of game-shooting lessons at a clay-pigeon instruction ground. Explain that you are a novice and need advice on both shooting driven birds and also etiquette. It will cost you, but it will be money very well spent. Driven pheasants can be amongst the most testing and difficult birds in the shooting field. Yes, on some low-ground, flat shoots the birds may prove relatively easy, though even here, new strains of pheasant can rocket sky high from the most level cover or gamecrop; but birds shown over deep valleys or from gamecrops surmounting a hill can humiliate even the most expert of shots. Many experienced game shots would probably agree that a lofty curling pheasant with the wind behind it figures high amongst the most baffling shots in the calendar.

The newcomer to driven shooting should, in my opinion, at all costs avoid the much lauded high bird shoots, many of which are to be found in the West Country. Some of the birds on these shoots will be driven from game crops or coverts on the summit of steep hills with the Guns way below, and will generally be flying at extreme range or even out of effective shot. Only experienced shots can deal with these birds, and they will be armed with tight chokes and heavy shot.

Inexperienced or moderate shots will find themselves completely out of their depth, frustrated and humiliated, quite apart from the fact that they may well send a number of birds on their way wounded and carrying shot. This type of occasion causes nothing but grief, not least amongst the pickers-up who have to try and recover every injured bird. For my part, I believe that these extremely high bird shoots, whilst they may carry a certain cachet and please a small number of skilful Shots, in the long term do the sport no favours.

OPPOSITE: *Views on the size of bags on a driven shoot can differ.*

But let's take a look at a typical day's driven shooting through the eyes of the gamekeeper, the man who has created the day through months of hard work and worry.

The Driven Day from the Gamekeeper's Perspective

The gamekeeper had been awake since 4am, restless and uneasy as the alarm clock ticked monotonously at his bedside. In two hours he would rise, but now he could only worry and fret over details, his mind ticking off, again and again, the agenda for the day that lay ahead. The beaters had been organized well over a month ago: it would be a full team of eighteen, for there was no sense in taking a chance on this, the first big shoot of the season. He was worried, though, about the youngsters. There were six of them today, all lads from the local village, cocky, self-assured and disinclined to listen to orders.

Still, he mused, he could trust his long-time reliable men. Jim, the oldest at seventy-nine, small, grizzled, and always shrouded in an ancient army greatcoat, could be trusted to keep the line straight. The remainder were all

Peg numbers being drawn.

sound and honest, working through the day with good humour and pungent wit. They knew their job and took pride in sending the birds over the line of Guns in steady streams, not in a tiresome dribble or a last minute flush of dozens of birds that would overwhelm the line.

They were people on whom he could rely. Take the brothers Johnston, for instance. Clad in old oilskins, thorn sticks grasped in knotted, purple hands, the pair would stop the long hedge on the first drive without a reminder, and by 8.30am they would be tapping away to turn back the cunning cock pheasants trying to break away from the main wood.

A clock struck the hour and the keeper rose, unable to keep company with his thoughts any longer. He dressed in the kitchen, leaving his wife still asleep, and slipped on his best tweeds, knotting his tie and wondering whether the weather would allow him to wear his leather boots, gleaming by the stove like polished chestnut.

Outside he glanced up. The sky was still black and clear, a waning moon hung above a distant wood, and there was a nip in the air, enough to hint at an early season frost; it promised to be a golden late autumn day. Only the labradors and springers in the kennels at the bottom of the yard broke the silence as they sensed movement. Back in the kitchen, a mug of tea to hand, he pondered on the day to come. How would the birds fly? Should be reasonable, he thought, for they were well grown even though the first time through is seldom brilliant.

At 9am the first Gun arrived, his car crunching up the gravel drive to the kennel yard. The promise of the dawn had been fulfilled, the sun glinting on oaks and beeches still clinging to leaves left after the early October gales. The grass was stiff with frost.

The team of beaters was already on their way to the first drive under the supervision of the under-keeper, a young man in his first job, while the two pickers-up, weatherbeaten ladies handling a brace each of golden retrievers and yellow labradors, were chatting to the gathering Guns. It was the same old team, syndicate members of some fifteen or so years and good shots on the whole, though inevitably there were a couple who could never get their act together. At the end of each shooting season they vowed to take shooting lessons in the summer, but they never did. It was, reflected the keeper, a puzzle. Why spend so much money and time for so little result? It annoyed him, too, for he hated the thought of wounded pheasants which should have been killed outright.

A buzz of chatter filled the yard as guns were placed in slips, cartridge bags filled and shooting sticks gathered up. As usual the host offered a tray of sloe gin, a glass to each Gun, pegs numbers were drawn and a token few words about safety and a reminder of a ban on shooting any ground game, such as rabbits and hares, was offered and then the team climbed into the shoot bus, a converted army lorry, to head for the first drive of the day.

The wood, crowning a small hill, was about twenty acres, with a long spur at one end which had already been blanked in. The line of pegs was 150 yards from the edge of the covert, and as each of the Guns reached his allotted peg he settled himself in, checked to see where the pickers-up were standing, and then loaded his gun. Several of the Guns wore cartridge belts with several cartridges raised from their loops for easy access, while other filled their jacket pockets.

A brief pause, silent, almost tangible, freezes the scene. The actors in the oft-repeated drama are still but alert. Each Gun has stamped a firm foothold by his peg and now stands prepared. A blackbird chinks in alarm, a blue-winged jay rasps a warning, sensing the hushed unease, and several pigeons swirl up from the woodland canopy.

A whistle from the far end of the wood starts the drive. The beaters swing into action, sticks tapping bushes and branches as they advance in line, whilst

Birds in the air...

bustling spaniels burst through the brambles. 'Cock forrard!' – the cry is clear in the crisp air and the Guns are all alert, each scanning the tree-tops in front. The pheasant has cork-screwed through the branches to gain height and power, curved wings flickering between glides. As it clears the wood, another and yet another bird is in the air.

For fifteen minutes each man concentrates on his immediate front as bird after bird powers across the line. Three Guns find themselves in a hot corner, hands frantically searching for fresh cartridges, breeches crisply opening and closing as puffs of blue smoke hang in the frosty air. Birds neatly killed and taken in front collapse as though struck by a giant fly-swatter, legs kicking as they thud to the ground behind the line. There is a smell of burnt powder, feathers drift on the slight breeze, and a spaniel runs in, unable to resist the temptation as a hen pheasant bounces on the ground yards from its nose.

Owl-like, a woodcock flickers out of the covert but escapes unscathed, missed by two Guns. The drive is nearly over, but a final flurry of birds erupts from the woodland and then, as the beaters appear, a whistle is blown and all shooting comes to a halt.

Nearly all the birds close to the line of Guns have been picked and only a young retriever circles its entreating master, reluctant to release its feathered prize. Way behind the line the pickers-up are searching for several runners and pricked birds.

The long weeks of spring and summer, the high hopes, the weather-dashed frustration, the hours of worry and hard graft, have culminated in these minutes of tension and drama. The keeper is suddenly aware of a sense of relief and pride in a job well done.

By lunchtime the bag stands at 165 pheasants, though the Guns prefer not to know, for each has £2 in the kitty as a wager on the total bag at the end of the day, half of which will be sent to the Countryside Alliance. The keeper joins the beaters in an ancient barn for a lunch of hot stew and beer, while the Guns gather in the farmhouse from which, an hour later, they emerge, chattering and jolly.

The last drive of the day is more a token gesture than a serious affair, the keeper quickly hurrying the beaters through a small copse beside a sluggish stream. Only six birds are shot, plus a mallard that flares up from the water, and now, as the sun sinks towards the horizon and the air turns colder, the vehicles wind back to the farmhouse. Tired dogs lean against legs, cartridge bags are almost empty and the chatter is of shots taken and birds killed or missed.

'Thank you, sir. Yes, they did fly well and we couldn't have wished for a better first time through.' The same time-honoured formula as a brace of pheasants and crisp notes change hands between keeper and Gun as each departs. The keeper drinks a cup of tea as the two pickers-up walk into the yard, each with a carrier holding several pheasants. 'That makes 186, sir, plus six various,' notes the under-keeper, 'and I dare say we'll pick three or four more tomorrow.'

The beaters and the pickers-up are paid and thanked, and the last brace of birds is hung. A few words with the under-keeper to arrange the morning's work and then, thank goodness, once the dogs have been checked for thorns and fed, the keeper knows he can relax by his fire, a glass of something warming to hand. Lights twinkle from the cottage window as he drives into the yard. For a brief moment he pauses by his vehicle, aware of the darkness and creeping tiredness, but content in the knowledge that, once again, he had achieved his goal: a good day's sport!

What to Wear?

Avoid at all costs the loud and ostentatious. Tweed jackets and breeches with glaring checks matched with brightly coloured socks are too often a sign of the tyro, the man who dresses to impress. If you are wearing a tweed outfit, then choose a quiet dark green or brown tweed, wear green stockings without coloured tops, don rubber boots or leather on a dry day, all topped off with a tweed cap or, as I prefer, a soft brown trilby. You may need a warm fleece or waistcoat on a bitterly cold day, and a rain- and windproof jacket. There are literally dozens such on the market today, each claiming the latest technology. Personally, I have worn the same dark green water- and windproof jacket, made in Finland, for over a decade, and it has served me well, both in the summer for stalking and in the winter for shooting and picking up. On a wet day you will also need a pair of water-proof over-trousers, while a towelling green or brown scarf will stop rain trickling down your neck.

As far as headgear is concerned, do not even contemplate wearing a base-ball-type cap, so beloved of Americans in the shooting field. It is a most inappropriate example of headwear, and has no place in the British shooting scene, though clay shooters seem to prefer it.

OPPOSITE: Over-trousers are essential on a wet day.

This, then is a typical day's driven shooting, but while the formula and the traditions will be second nature to experienced Guns, the day itself can present a formidable series of hazards and potential *faux-pas* to the newcomer to the sport.

A Day's Driven Shooting from the Gun's Perspective

You have booked a day's driven shooting or have had an invitation, and now the great day has arrived. Make sure you have more than enough cartridges, and if you are in any doubt ask your host how many to bring. You will have an indication of the anticipated bag to give you a clue, but as already mentioned, nothing is more embarrassing than to find yourself running short of cartridges on a drive. It is an insult to your host.

The majority of shoots meet at 9am and it is essential to be on time. Nothing looks worse than to make a late entrance or hold up the other Guns. Often there will be coffee, or even a light breakfast, requiring an even earlier arrival time. Your host will welcome everyone and outline the format for the day. He will almost certainly emphasize safety at all costs, point out that no ground game is to be shot, and explain the numbering system for the day.

Make sure you have enough cartridges for the day.

Every shoot adopts its own methods, but numbering from the right or left and moving up two at each drive is fairly standard. I have, however, attended some shoots that seem to take a perverse pleasure in inflicting a complicated technique on the team. Some shoots now provide each Gun with a card indicating the drives and the numbering on each.

To Shoot, and What Not to Shoot

Today, grey partridges have suffered such a drastic decline in numbers that where they do still exist, mingling with redlegs, most shoots ask Guns to make a point of not shooting them. For the beginner this can be daunting, though the flight and call is very different to that of the French partridge. In addition, a small number of shoots prefer not to shoot woodcock, though in my opinion this is totally misguided as numbers are holding up well.

Where woodcock are reasonably abundant there is always the faint chance of achieving a right-and-left at these elusive birds. If you do achieve the feat

A grouse being taken well in front.

you will be eligible for membership of the prestigious *Shooting Times* Woodcock Club, but you will require two witnesses to your deed, and furthermore, your gun must not leave your shoulder between shots!

Once you are on your peg and have removed your gun from its sleeve, settle down to look around you. Behind you may see pickers-up with their dogs, and you should try to remember where they are placed. Note your neighbouring Guns, load, and then wait for the whistle or horn, which indicates the drive is under way. Make sure you are standing comfortably with your gun under your arm, but keep alert. Today, some Guns seem to prefer to wait for birds with their guns open, a ridiculous habit, which ensures that the gun has to be closed before it can be brought to the shoulder. It's a waste of time and has no safety value.

On a driven pheasant day if a bird is heading towards your killing zone, try to shoot it in front. So many Guns seem almost mesmerized by an oncoming bird and wait until it is almost overhead before swinging into action. They then miss, and turn round to take a going-away shot, which again misses or pricks the bird. The experienced and accomplished shot will make it all look so easy with minimum movement and a dead bird falling in front of, or just behind, his peg.

Do not, under any circumstances, 'poach' your neighbour's birds, and if you do inadvertently kill a bird that should have been his, a quick apology is called for. A cardinal sin, and one likely to elicit a request to remove yourself from the scene, is to shoot down the line of Guns. This is highly dangerous and could result in a severe accident. In similar fashion make sure that you always shoot at sky and never into the tree-line, especially when beaters are approaching the end of a drive. It is all a matter of commonsense and being able to appreciate the rules of safety.

Should You Bring Your Gundog With You?

Personally, and as one who spends a great deal of time picking up with labradors, I cannot see the point of a Gun having a dog with him. The animal may be perfectly trained to sit, without a restraint, behind the peg, but all it will be required to do at the end of a drive is collect a handful of birds in the immediate area of its master, birds which could have been picked by hand. The team of pickers-up are on hand to collect the bag and, on occasion, resent Guns' dogs interfering with their work.

At the end of the day, when the Guns foregather to discuss the bag and perhaps enjoy a late lunch or high tea, each will be presented by the keeper with a brace of birds and, in exchange, money will change hands. How much? Well, the amount does vary from shoot to shoot and according to the bag size. The answer is to have a quiet word with your host to check the form.

Thank the beaters for their hard work.

Thank the Beaters

Don't neglect to thank the team of beaters for all their hard work. So often Guns seem to forget the fact that their sport would not exist were it not for ten or twenty men, women and youngsters who are prepared to walk all day, uphill and down dale, through the thickest cover, and to work their dogs in order to ensure a good day's sport. Simply to drive away without a verbal appreciation for their efforts is unforgivable. The same applies to the pickers-up, who will have worked their dogs throughout the day and made sure that every last bird was accounted for. No shoot can operate without the assistance of these men and women with their well trained gundogs. It is their duty to see that wounded birds, however far they may fly before dropping, are collected and despatched, and the Guns owe them a debt of gratitude.

In Summary

The driven shoot is often the target of ignorant criticism, particularly from those opposed to any form of shooting. Opponents will, in their ignorance, claim that birds are tame and can all too easily be 'blasted out of the sky'. However, those who know the sport, and so know what they are talking about, will confirm that high-flying pheasants, curling with the wind behind them, are amongst the most difficult birds of all to shoot.

11
Gundogs

Owning a competent, working gundog, of whatever breed, is a constant source of great pleasure and, for most aspects of shooting, a vital necessity. For the rough shooter, the pigeon specialist and most certainly for the wildfowler, a capable gundog is absolutely essential, not simply to retrieve the bag but also to ensure that any wounded bird or animal is brought to hand for swift despatch. The one exception to the rule is the driven game Shot who spends his or her entire season standing at a peg, confident in the knowledge that all birds, dead or pricked, will be gathered by the team of pickers-up armed with well trained and seasoned dogs.

However, you can guarantee that one or more Guns on a driven day will have a dog with them at the peg, and that all too often it will be attached to a metal corkscrew device to stop it running in. Occasionally, a well trained retriever may be seen sitting quietly behind its owner, waiting for the end of the drive to pick any birds close to hand – but this is the exception, and frankly it is not really necessary to have a dog present to collect birds that can be picked by hand. I have even seen a dog connected to its owner by a lead, despite the fact that he was shooting – a sure recipe for disaster. I can well understand wanting to bring along a faithful, well loved gundog on a driven day, but unless it is totally steady, then it makes more sense to leave it at home and to concentrate on the shooting in the knowledge that all birds will be gathered by the pickers-up.

Over the years I have owned, trained and worked spaniels, a German shorthaired pointer and a series of yellow Labradors, and I can't imagine being without the companionship of a capable gundog. In the past I have rented a small shoot where the hedges were broad and dense and the gutters broad and deep, where without a dog one would not expect to recover even a quarter of the anticipated seasonal bag, while flighting duck at dusk would be a waste of time: in the deepening gloom a shot bird, thumping into the reeds, would be all but impossible to recover by hand. Furthermore, without a dog I would rarely have been able to turn out the occasional hedgerow pheasant: I needed that snuffling nose to tell me that a bird was to hand, and the thrusting head to eject it skywards.

If at all feasible, anyone who shoots on a regular basis, with the possible exception of the driven Shot, should make every effort to own a capable gundog. Without one you have to rely on your companions, with the result that the bag and the sport will be reduced. Certainly, no one contemplating wildfowling should step on to the foreshore without the assistance of a strong, experienced dog, unless they go out with a companion wildfowler who owns such an animal.

Choosing a Gundog

Breed

The question of breed selection is critical for the first-time owner, and must be linked to the type of shooting he or she expects to have, in conjunction with his or her domestic circumstances. Today the working gundog world in Britain is full to capacity with different breeds, many of them newcomers from the Continent, and each with its loyal band of followers. But this book is aimed at the beginner, so for simplicity's sake I would strongly recommend the choice of a springer spaniel for rough and walked-up shooting, and a

My personal choice is a Labrador.

Labrador for wildfowling and game shooting. This is only a broad general-ization, for many individuals will use a Labrador as a maid-of-all-work, and I have personally owned springers that were adapt at handling walked-up hedgerow and thick cover sport, yet equally could just about tolerate the slower pace of a driven day when picking up.

I have also owned and handled a German shorthaired pointer, a dog that was a joy to shoot over. In the field he was staunch on point, flushed his game on command, and retrieved to hand, while as an asset for deer stalking he was unbeatable. Walking a pace or two in front of me, he would at once tell me if a roe was nearby, while on the thankfully few occasions when I had a wounded animal, he was brilliant at tracking and letting me know when he had found his quarry.

The selection and choice of a first gundog is critical. The animal will hope-fully be an active and useful companion for ten or more working years, and must not only meet your shooting requirements, but also fit into the domes-tic scene. My personal choice would be a Labrador, rather than a springer, assuming that you intend to train the dog yourself. Springers and cockers are both outstanding working breeds, but can prove to be a handful for the novice owner and trainer. Energetic, bustling and delighting in hard work, they require a handler who is able to control their exuberance to ensure they work within a reasonably close pattern. A dog that constantly pulls ahead to flush game out of range is a liability.

Today, there is a wide choice of gundog breeds from which to select, including a number of Continental breeds. The HPRs (hunters, pointers, retrievers) such as the German shorthaired pointer, the Brittany spaniel, Weimaraners, Vizslas and Large and Small Munsterlanders, all have an enthusiastic following and in competent hands can prove to be extremely effective.

Dog or Bitch?

Whatever breed of gundog you decide on, whether you intend to buy a puppy and train it yourself, or go to the expense of having it professionally trained, there are several essential ground rules to be considered. Firstly, are you looking for a dog or a bitch? Experience over the years has taught me that bitches tend to be easier to train and handle than dogs. They have a softer, more amenable nature, whereas a dog, whilst it may have more drive and display more energy in the field than a bitch, also has the disad-vantage of being easily distracted by bitches, even though they are not in season.

However, bitches do have the disadvantage of coming into season twice a year, for three weeks at a time, and you can almost guarantee that the animal will be out of action for at least a part of the shooting season and, of course, cannot be taken out in public. Nevertheless, looking ahead, you may wish eventually to breed from your bitch with a view to retaining a puppy to continue the line. I have found that keeping a dog and bitch under the same roof is not at all difficult if commonsense is used. I bred from my yellow Labrador bitch when she was six, and from a litter of eight kept back a dog puppy which I have trained to pick up and work alongside his mother.

Kennel Club Registered

Selecting a puppy to be your shooting companion for the next ten or more years is critical. It is essential to know the working background of both sire and dam, and ideally, to see them in action. Both must have Kennel Club pedigrees, which you can examine, and even if the kennel names going back five generations mean little to you, you can at least assess the number of field trial champions and winners there are in it. Ideally there will be no show blood in the lines. Sadly, the showing fraternity has wrecked the working ability of so many gundog breeds by concentrating on appearance rather than ability in the field. Indeed, some breeds are now little more than travesties of the genuine article. Show English springers today bear little resemblance to the genuine working dog, displaying long ears and too much feather, features that would hamper their ability to work in thick cover, even if they retained any drive.

In selecting a puppy do not simply pick one from a litter bred by a friend up the road, or one that comes at a suspiciously low price and lacks any paperwork or pedigree. Don't allow emotion to over-rule commonsense. A litter of puppies may look adorable, but if the parents are not registered with the Kennel Club, then if you later decide to breed a litter yourself you may have great difficulty selling the puppies as they cannot be registered.

Selecting a Puppy

Assuming, however, that you have found a breeder with a litter that takes your eye, and where the pedigrees on both sides display working and not show blood, then selection of a puppy is critical. Ideally, both parents will be of good working stock and regularly used in the field. If you are able, make enquiries from third parties who have seen the parents working, and make sure they carry no faults such as hard mouth, yapping in the field, nervousness or aggression. It is, of course, not always possible to discover the working abilities and traits of the parents, but if you can obtain copies of the pedigrees on both sides and show them to a seasoned gundog trainer or owner, you will be able to absorb some impartial advice.

Picking a suitable puppy from a litter is not easy. At seven or eight weeks the pups should be lively and look well in themselves. Choose a bold little puppy, one that looks you in the eye, has the coat colour and markings you seek, and is of the sex you require. Ideally it will be a spring litter, as you will then have the summer to house-train the youngster and instil some very basic training.

How Much to Pay?

What should you expect to pay today for a gundog puppy, a Labrador or springer, with a good pedigree and from working parents? Well, I would not expect to see much change from £500 to £700, and I would be suspicious if the asking price were considerably less. If the dog is not Kennel Club registered then you can expect to pay considerably less, but it is always better to know that both parents are KC registered, and to this end, as I have said before, you should be able to examine the pedigrees on either side. Look out for Field Trial Champions, marked as FTCh, and also FT winners, but look with askance at a pedigree containing Show Champions. One or two may just be acceptable, but no more.

Do not be tempted by adult dogs that are being offered free 'to good homes'. There is usually no such thing as a 'free' dog. Why is it being given away? Is it aggressive to strangers and children, does it constantly bark, does it destroy its home patch? Avoid it and let someone else sort out the animal's problems.

You can, of course, buy a half or fully trained dog from a professional trainer, but be aware that the price will be commensurate with the animal's ability and background. If you do go along this route, make sure that you see the dog working, ideally on a shoot, and also make a careful note of all the commands used by the trainer. Even acquire exactly the same whistle that he or she uses.

Remember, too, that the dog will be leaving its adult home and all that it knows for a new world and owner. Do not, under any circumstance, take the animal out shooting or picking up as soon as it is acquired, but rather let it settle in for several weeks in order to get to know you and its fresh surroundings before embarking on real work.

Characteristics to Choose

As to selection of a pup from a litter of four- or five-week-old captivating wrigglers, each looking adorable, this is where, too often, heart rules over head. In the case of a Labrador I would look for a broad head, dark eyes, a double coat and a thick otter tail. Select a bold little pup that moves well and has straight legs and a kind expression, and if possible, see not only the mother but the sire as well. Both will give you an indication of the manner in which the puppy should develop. Unfortunately, today there are too many small, rakish Labradors with narrow, snipey heads, thin coats and whippety tails. This type of dog should be avoided at all costs.

A puppy is going to be a working companion for the best part of a decade, and it should not be chosen in haste, nor should your heart be ruled by emotion. Look at several litters and engage the assistance of a knowledgeable friend before making a decision.

Bringing the Puppy Home

The puppy itself can be taken from the litter at eight weeks old. Before collection you should acquire a large cage and line it with either paper or Vet-Bed, a soft rug-like material. Remember that separation from its mother and siblings will be a dramatic event for the puppy. Let the little dog enjoy a biscuit or two in the cage, and then let it out so that it begins to associate the cage with home. Bring along some old bedding from its first home, so that it can begin to associate it with a degree of familiarity. Make sure that water is always readily available, together with some toys; when the dog is about four or five months old it can then have a bone or two to chew.

When you come to name your dog, give careful thought to what can be a tricky subject. The animal will, we hope, be Kennel Club registered and have its own KC name, which will almost certainly be elaborate. I prefer a working name with two syllables as this creates more emphasis, but do not include 'no' at the end of the name, as this will inevitably create confusion in the dog's mind. 'No' is a key training word, so a dog called Beano may quickly become confused when you shout 'Bea. . . no!'

Training

Can the amateur, even a first-time owner, train a gundog to a satisfactory level in the shooting field, whether for hunting and flushing game, or working as a peg dog or for picking up? The answer is a categorical yes, provided

A young springer showing great promise.

intelligence and commonsense are employed. Today, there are numerous CDs on the market dealing with every aspect of gundog training, and these, used in conjunction with a good training manual, should enable the novice trainer to produce his dog to a perfectly acceptable level of training for the shooting field.

Sadly, however, one still sees gundogs that will not walk to heel, which run in, refuse to deliver a dummy or bird, or ignore the whistle. These misdeeds are not the fault of the animal, but can be attributed to idle, half-hearted training on the part of the owner.

My advice to a beginner who wishes to train their first gundog themselves, is to purchase two books, backed up by training CDs. The books are *In the Bag – Labrador Training from Puppy to Gundog* by Margaret Allen and *Gundog Training for the Home and Field* by Paul Rawlings (both published by Crowood). Both books are essential reading and will provide the novice trainer with all the information they need to produce a fully trained dog for the field.

In addition, the beginner should make a point of attending gundog training classes. Here, not only will the young dog begin its learning curve, but it will also associate with other dogs and learn civilized behaviour, while its handler will be instructed in the training process, in teaching the dog to sit, walk to heel, stay and come to whistle. The basic elements of gundog training, and every stage thereafter, must be thoroughly learnt and absorbed by the dog and understood by its handler. Too often a novice trainer will rush through basic training in order to achieve the more exciting aspects of dummy retrieving – and suddenly the dog is pulling ahead and no longer walking correctly to heel, or running in when a dummy is thrown.

Formal training may start when the puppy is around six months old, but from day one every aspect of the puppy's life can involve an aspect of training. When being fed the youngster must be taught to sit and wait before being allowed to eat, it must learn its name, and even as a small puppy, a thrown handkerchief or soft rubber ball can be used to provide play retrieves. Formal training sessions, once you feel the youngster is old enough, should be relatively short and clear-cut. You may not have ideal conditions close by for training, but basic work can readily be achieved in an enclosed garden.

A Labrador steady during a grouse drive.

The choice of sex is very important. Currently, as I have written above, I have two yellow Labradors, one a bitch and the other her puppy, a dog, chosen from a litter of eight, which she had after a carefully selected mating. The bitch was easy to train, very amenable and always compliant. Her puppy, now four as I write, is more ebullient and needs a firm hand, but has also proved excellent in the field. Both dogs are used largely for picking up on driven shoots, and are worked as a team. There has been no problem managing the two in the same premises: I use an outside kennel for the dog, and the bitch sleeps in the house, and I make sure that neither meets during the critical period. However, I would recommend that the novice owner sticks to one dog to start with!

Training your own gundog is not rocket science, but it does require commonsense, patience, and an understanding of a dog's thinking process and ability to understand what you are trying to impart. Never, ever lose patience or your temper with a dog you are trying to train. If things are not going right, call a halt to the lesson, calm down, and leave it until the next day. Shouting and frightening your charge will set back the training programme and may result in a dog that will no longer trust you.

Your pupil must learn that you are the pack leader, and it should want to be with you at all times. The relationship between trainer and dog is subtle and immensely satisfying, and there is nothing more satisfying than producing a well trained gundog for the shooting field, from a tiny eight-week-old puppy.

12
Dealing with the Bag

With the obvious exception of pest birds such as the corvid tribe (though young rooks or branchers can be fashioned into a reasonable pie), what you shoot you should be prepared to eat, and that includes grey squirrels – which are extremely tasty and well worth the rather fiddly preparation. All game, feathered or furred – and in my book that includes wildfowl, pigeons, rabbits as well as hares – is greatly to be preferred to reared meat. It is lean, has fed on natural food, lived a healthy albeit relatively brief life, and, as an added bonus, is readily accessible during the shooting season. It can also be frozen for a year or so (though should not be left so long that skin burn takes place).

Game, in the sense of pheasants and red-leg partridges, is now at last becoming increasingly popular, largely due to the 'Game to eat' campaign launched by the Countryside Alliance, with the result that supermarkets are now marketing dressed birds in season, while old-fashioned butchers have long catered for this market. The problem with both pheasants and partridges is that they are surrounded by a myth. Game, we are told, must be hung until it falls off the hook and the flesh, when plucked, has assumed a pleasing shade of greenish purple! This is, of course, quite unnecessary and you can, if you wish, eat your pheasant the day after it was shot. It will, admittedly, veer towards a bland flavour rather than the tangy game taste it will acquire if it has been hung for a week or so, but this is entirely up to individual choice.

Much depends on the weather and the time of year. Partridges shot in a warm September, if they are to be hung for two or three days, must be protected from blow-flies and suspended in a netting cage, making sure that the feathers are isolated from the covering as flies can lay their eggs through the smallest of netting holes. The ideal situation is a cool, dry shed with a roof beam to which a dozen or so hooks can be attached. Both pheasants and partridges can be suspended by the neck, though there is a school of thought which maintains that by hanging the bird by one leg, air can circulate round the vent, while the entrails drop back into the body to flavour the flesh. Again, the choice is yours!

Preparing a Bird for the Table

There is a choice when it comes to plucking or dismantling your pheasant or partridge. The easy way is simply to remove the breast meat and discard the rest. Slit the skin down the centre of the breast, stopping at the base of the breastbone; pull the skin down on either side, exposing the meat, which can then be cut off in two entire sections.

For my part, however, the end result of filleting is never as satisfactory as a plucked bird, carefully dressed and roasted. Plucking is, I have to admit, a chore, but even so the final presentation is always far more satisfactory than two lumps of skinless meat. Ideally, plucking is always at its easiest while a bird is still warm, though this, of course, is totally impractical. It takes about thirty minutes to pluck a pheasant completely, starting with the wings, then the tail and moving on to the breast. Initially, where the body is concerned, hold the bird by the neck and just pluck upwards two or three feathers at a time. If you try and pull a bunch of feathers downwards you will almost certainly tear the skin. Go carefully and steadily. There will probably be a layer of fat on either side of the breast, and here the skin can easily be torn.

Once the bird is completely denuded of feathers, then the entrails must be removed. Make a horizontal slit across the skin below the breast bone, insert

A well dressed pheasant ready for the table.

your hand into the cavity, and pull out the entrails, lungs, heart and kidneys. If you are squeamish, put on a thin rubber surgical glove. When plucking a duck you may find that even when you have removed all the feathers, there still remains a fine stubble; this can be removed by singeing the body with matches.

Once the bird, whether pheasant, partridge, pigeon or duck, has been plucked and cleaned, it should then be trussed. This not only makes it easier to carve, but also makes the end result look attractive. With the bird lying breast down, make a slit at the base of the neck, cutting upwards for one or two inches, depending on the bird's size, then slice through the base of the neck and windpipe, pull them upwards and cut off the skin beneath them. Pull back the loose flap of skin to cover the hole you have made, and bring back each wing close to the body: then secure all with a skewer through one wing, the body and into the other wing. Turn the bird over, and wind a piece of string round the base of the legs and the parson's nose and tie it tightly. With snipe and woodcock, a cocktail stick thrust horizontally through each leg will hold them in place.

Grouse, Woodcock and Snipe

Grouse, woodcock and snipe are delicious birds on the table and are much sought after. They must always be fully plucked and carefully prepared. Where woodcock is concerned the traditionalist will leave the entrails (the trail) in the bird, and break the legs at the knee to remove the sinews. Woodcock or snipe should then be wrapped in a rasher of bacon, smeared with butter and cooked under a grill for ten minutes. The bacon is then removed and set aside, and the bird returned to the oven for a further five minutes when the trail can be scooped out.

Now chop the bacon finely and mix it with the trail, add some lemon juice, pepper and salt, and spread the mixture on a slice of toast. Serve the bird on the toast and spoon pan juices over it. Delicious!

To my mind, where cooking game is concerned, whilst game cookbooks offer a variety of recipes, such as pheasant joints in crumbs, pheasant in tomato sauce, or stewed pheasant with sauerkraut, you cannot beat pheasant, partridge or grouse simply roasted. Smear the breast of a bird with butter and a drizzle of olive oil, put a dollop of butter, a lemon wedge or half an onion inside the cavity, pepper and salt the bird well, and cover the breast with streaky bacon. Roast for thirty-five minutes at 190°C, then remove the bacon and set aside to keep warm; return the bird to the oven for a further ten minutes to make sure the breast skin is crispy brown. Serve with whatever takes your fancy: Brussels sprouts, young potatoes, watercress or perhaps game chips.

This recipe can be used for all the gamebirds, wildfowl and woodpigeons, but if you do want to experiment, then don't be constrained by convention. If you want to curry birds, marinate them, make a terrine, or cook them in wine and orange, feel free!

Woodpigeon

Never turn up your nose at humble fare! Woodpigeons, particularly young birds of the year, distinguished by the lack of a white neck ring, are excellent when roasted. In early autumn the birds are plump and fat from living on spilt harvest grain, though in hard weather, especially in winter when green crops are snow covered, the birds may be thin and scarcely worth a culinary effort.

One great advantage offered by woodpigeon is the fact that their feathers are loose, so much so that a bird can be fully plucked in less than two minutes. Indeed, there was a time when BASC ran woodpigeon plucking competitions at the CLA Game Fair, with some extraordinary times being recorded.

They can be roasted, or you can make pigeon terrine, casserole a brace of birds, stew them or cook with apples, apricots or haricot beans. Once again, there is no constraint on your imagination!

Rabbit

The humble rabbit is too often overlooked, yet this animal is delicious on the table and neglected only by the ignorant and by some elderly country folk who tell you they've never eaten a rabbit since myxomatosis! Young, three-quarter-grown rabbits are ideal for the kitchen, and should never be hanged. The animal is always paunched as soon as it has been shot or ferreted. Before this is done the bladder is emptied of any urine by pressing the belly downwards with the thumb. The simplest way to remove the entrails is to make a slit in the skin from the sternum to the vent and then, holding the back legs and forelegs in each hand, give a sharp flick and the entrails will shoot out, leaving the kidneys and liver behind.

Skinning is simple: cut a semi-circle in the skin, from side to side in the centre of the body, and then with each hand grasping a section of skin, pull sideways. Cut off the head, tail and lower legs, wash in cold water, pat dry, and set aside for cooking.

Rabbit has a relatively mild flavour, and is not nearly as gamey as hare. Again there are numerous ways of treating the meat, but my favourite is rabbit stew. Most recipes will suggest that you joint the rabbit before cooking; however, I prefer to cut the meat away from the leg, the back and even the small fillets inside the carcase, and the meat can then be marinated in cider for several hours. To cook, place the meat into a stew pan along with the cider, chopped-up onions, some lightly fried mushrooms, 4oz of diced ham and two or three potatoes also chopped up. Add some stock, salt and pepper, and cook for two or three hours over a low heat until everything is tender. Accompany with a good French red wine.

Another way with rabbit is to select a half-grown youngster and then pan fry the legs and meat from the back, having sprinkled it well with flour. If you can add some freshly picked field mushrooms and streaky bacon you will have an unbeatable breakfast!

Hare

The brown hare is treated in a very different fashion to the rabbit and can really be classed as game. It is not, for instance, immediately paunched in the field, but is allowed to hang in a cool, dry, fly-free situation for at least a week. There is then the slightly unpleasant task of removing the innards and collecting the blood for gravy. Great care must be taken not to puncture the entrails: make a clean skin cut along the belly, then work the skin back along the hind legs. Cut round the tail and work the skin down the back towards the head and down the front legs. Then cut off the head.

Now carefully slit the belly containing the entrails and remove them, retaining the liver and kidneys. Slice through the rib-cage and retain any blood that has pooled there. Cut away the membrane on either side of the body, then wash the hare and let it soak in salted water for two or three hours.

Hare is a strong, extremely tasty meat, and in my opinion, best enjoyed as the classic jugged hare recipe served with redcurrant jelly and a powerful red wine. Correctly prepared, it is a dish worthy of a king. Here is a recipe that I have stolen from my old friend, the late Fred Taylor's highly practical book, *One for the Pot* (A. & C. Black). Never one to get too excited about exact quantities or picky methods of preparation, for jugged hare Fred advises as follows:

Cut all the meat from the hare and then pressure cook the bones with onions, carrots, mixed herbs and beef stock cubes to make a concentrated stock of about 1½ pints for a normal-sized hare. Then roll the hare meat in seasoned flour and fry to a golden brown in hot butter.

Now place the meat in a crock or stone pickle jar and cover with the stock. Add two whole onions spiked with six cloves, add a squeeze of lemon juice, a bay leaf and a glass of port or red wine. Cover the container and bake slowly at around 190°C for around three hours. Serve with redcurrant jelly.

Personally, I would add two or three glasses of port or wine to give it an extra kick. Yummy!

Wildfowl

As far as wildfowl are concerned, and particularly duck, flavour greatly depends on what the bird has been eating. Duck shot inland, particularly stubble-fed mallard, are usually delicious, but birds that have been feeding on the foreshore may be tainted with a muddy or fishy flavour. Inland teal are one of my favourite ducks in both the sporting and table sense. Flighting fast at dusk or rocketing high from a drain, these little duck provide outstanding sport and are delicious on the table.

It is some considerable time since I last shot a goose, and that was a singularly ancient Canada which succumbed to two barrels on the Exe estuary in Devon. It was a nightmare to pluck and proved leathery and tasteless on the table. However, a young goose, be it a pinkfoot, greylag or whitefront (which may only be shot in England and is protected in Scotland), is a very different story. The flesh tends to be dark and usually lacks any fat, for these are muscular birds which may fly a considerable distance to feed inland on pasture, stubble or winter wheat.

Advocates of wild goose on the table claim that the bird must be hung for anything up to three weeks or more, depending on the weather and the prevalence of flies, but I would certainly choose no more than a week. The Canada goose is the heaviest of the wild geese, but remember that all the geese species give the illusion of being larger than they actually are once de-feathered, and the amount of meat available may prove disappointing, especially if you are having a dinner party!

Once again my preference is for straightforward roast goose. Make sure you have a young bird and cook it for up to three hours, basting it regularly with juice from the pan mixed with stock in order to ensure the meat does not dry out.

Incidentally, it is illegal to sell wild geese, so unless you are a wildfowler operating in an area where geese are present, you will have to rely on the generosity of friends for a grey goose. This, however, does not apply to parts of Scotland, such as Orkney and the Uists, due to the need to cull large numbers of feral greylags. As a result goose meat may be sold locally under licence.

Canadas are now found countrywide, and frequently inland, and have, in some instances become such a pest through fouling and crop damage that they can now be shot year round under general licence. Make sure, however, before taking any action out of the normal shooting season for wildfowl, that you have read and understood the terms of the licence.

Afterword

There is a type of shooting man for whom the essence of the sport and the quality of a day's shooting is dictated solely by the number of birds shot at the end of the day. 'Oh yes,' he will modestly recount, 'we had a decent day, killed 300 birds and they flew quite well, but with a better team we could have topped 400 or more.' Numbers, simply numbers, and to him the birds were little more than targets . . . clay pigeons with wings, and the more the merrier. Does he express any interest in the keeper's year, how the birds are produced for his sport? The beaters and the pickers-up are simply a dimension of the entire exercise, which, as far as he is concerned, is calculated to ensure he fires as many shots as possible.

The genuine shooting man will take an interest in all aspects of keepering, will understand how the shooting year works, and take a deep and genuine interest in wildlife, conservation and the rural year. Shooting has a role to play, but it is only a part of the whole.

Legal Information

Shooting Seasons for Gamebirds

Grouse	12 August to 10 December
Ptarmigan	12 August to 10 December
Black game	20 August to 10 December
Pheasant	1 October to 1 February
Partridge	1 September to 1 February

Birds in Schedule 2 of the Wildlife & Countryside Act 1981, which may be killed or taken outside the close season, and which may be sold dead from 1 September to 28 February:

Coot	1 September to 31 January
Common snipe	12 August to 31 January
Woodcock (England/Wales)	1 October to 31 January
(Scotland)	1 September to 31 January
Golden plover	1 September to 31 January
Tufted duck	Above the high-water mark of ordinary
Mallard	spring tides 1 September to 31 January.
Pochard	Below the high-water mark of ordinary
Shoveler	spring tides 1 September to 20 February
Teal	
Wigeon	

Note: While snipe may be shot in August, they may not be sold dead until September.

Birds in Schedule 2 of the Wildlife and Countryside Act 1981 which may be killed or taken outside the close season, but which may not be sold dead:

Canada goose	Above the high-water mark
Greylag goose	of ordinary spring tides
	1 September to 31 January

Pinkfooted goose	Below the high-water mark
White-fronted goose (except in Scotland)	of ordinary spring tides
Gadwall	1 September to 20 February
Goldeneye	
Moorhen	1 September to 31 January

Birds That May be Shot or Trapped at Any Time

The birds listed here may be shot or trapped at any time under general licence; note that some of the birds listed may not be controlled for as wide a range of reasons as others. It is therefore essential to read and understand individual licences:

In England, Scotland and Wales: Crow (carrion and hooded), collared dove, rook, woodpigeon, Canada goose, magpie, feral pigeon, jay, jackdaw, ruddy duck
Additionally in England: Egyptian goose, lesser black-backed gull, ring-necked parakeet, monk parakeet
In Scotland: Great black-backed gull, lesser black-backed gull

Note that only woodpigeon may be sold dead. Other species may be given away. Also the licences issued for shooting ruddy duck and monk parakeets are for the purpose of eradicating the species in the wild, rather than controlling them.

Gamekeepers and anyone in England and Wales troubled by herring gulls and great black-backed gulls should apply for individual licences well before damage is expected to occur. In Scotland, lesser black-backed and herring gulls may only be shot for public health and similar reasons, and individual licences are required.

Note, however, that a review of all wildlife legislation may result in new legislation.

Lead Shot

In England and Wales the use of lead shot is currently prohibited in the following circumstances:

- On or over any area below the high water mark of ordinary spring tides
- On or over designated Sites of Special Scientific Interests (SSSIs)
- For shooting moorhen, coot and any species of duck or goose anywhere

The effect of this legislation makes it illegal to use lead shot cartridges to shoot pest species or game in areas 1 and 2 listed above.

In Scotland the law prohibits the use of cartridges loaded with lead shot on or over wetlands. This includes pest control and game shooting. Wetland is defined as marshland, peatland, fen, water, whether static or flowing, permanent or temporary and including marine water the depth of which at low tide does not exceed six metres. However, ducks, geese and other legal quarry may be shot with lead shot over land which is not wetland.

Non-Lead Shot

A variety of non-lead shot is now available, including steel and bismuth, but anyone using a shotgun, particularly an older gun, should consult a gunsmith before using non-lead cartridges, particularly steel. Elderly game guns may not be suitable. It is absolutely essential that non-lead shot cartridges are used to shoot wildfowl and to comply with current regulations. Non-compliance could eventually lead to the banning of all lead shot, irrespective of quarry or area.

Shooting on or Near a Highway

Despite belief to the contrary, there is no prohibition on shooting within 50ft (15m) of a highway. However, in England and Wales it is an offence to fire a shot within 50ft of the centre of a highway if a user on the highway is injured, interrupted or endangered. A highway is defined as any road over which the public has a right of way in a vehicle. However, a bridleway, footpath or cycle way is not a highway. However, one should never shoot close to a path being used by the public, nor can you shoot on a public road or its verge.

In Scotland, whilst it is accepted that one can shoot from a public highway, under common law reckless discharge of a firearm would apply if disturbance or inconvenience was caused to the public.

Selling and Possession of Game

In England and Wales, provided they were lawfully killed during the open season, game and woodpigeons may be bought or sold at any time of the year. Hares, on the other hand, may not be sold between March and July inclusive. The following birds may only be sold dead from 1 September to 28 February: coot, snipe, woodcock, golden plover, tufted duck, mallard, pintail, pochard, shoveller, teal, wigeon.

In Scotland dead wild birds, including game, may be bought or sold at any time of the year, provided they were lawfully killed during the open season. Hares may not be sold in the close season. The birds listed above under England and Wales – i.e. coot, snipe, etc. – may also only be sold from 1 September to 28 February.

Gun Security

Whether you own one shotgun or several, a gun cabinet is the ideal method of ensuring your guns are secure whenever they are not in use. A cabinet should be securely fixed to a wall in a situation where it is out of sight of visitors. It should not be in a garage or any outside building. The keys to the cabinet must be hidden in a location known only to the certificate holder. Shotgun ammunition does not have to be secured in a cabinet but common-sense requires that it is kept in a location where it is not readily accessible to anyone other than the gun owner. Cartridges should not be stored where there is a risk of fire, such as a kitchen.

When travelling with a gun(s) never, under any circumstances, leave it unattended in an unlocked car, if only for a matter of minutes. If a gun is left in a vehicle, it should be out of sight and the car locked. In public, guns must always be carried in a case or slip, and if you are, for instance, having lunch in a pub, remove a gun's fore-end and keep it on your person. Vigilance at all times is essential, as thieves can strike swiftly. Incidentally, hospitality on some shoots can be a trifle excessive and it is an offence to be drunk in charge of a loaded gun.

Shotgun Possession Age Limits

There is no minimum age at which a person may be lent a shotgun or obtain a shotgun certificate. However, a person under the age of fifteen with an assembled shotgun must be under the supervision of a person aged at least twenty-one, unless the gun is in a securely fastened cover so that it cannot be fired. Persons under the age of fifteen cannot buy or be given a shotgun, but they may be lent one.

Between the ages of fifteen to seventeen one may purchase or hire a shotgun and ammunition. The minimum age at which one may purchase or hire a shotgun is eighteen.

Despatching Wounded Game

Anyone who shoots for sport has a duty to know how to swiftly and humanely despatch a wounded bird or ground game. On game shoots one

Despatching a wounded bird with a priest.

still occasionally sees the clumsy head-twirling method of trying to kill a wounded pheasant. Unfortunately, unless one is very skilful, the result can be hopelessly unpleasant, particularly for the unfortunate bird. In addition, if either this method, or the method of breaking the neck by stretching it with the head bent back, is used, it makes it difficult to tie the bird by the now elongated neck.

The answer is to use a priest, a small weighted club used to 'give the last rites' – hence the name. Hand-made priests can be bought from sporting stores, or you can easily make your own, using either a roe-deer leg bone, cleaned and dried, or a wooden shaft weighted at one end with molten lead poured into a drilled-out cavity. A wounded bird can be killed instantly with a sharp blow to the head. If you are working one or two dogs and spend most of your time picking up, then a priest is an essential item of equipment. An alternative to a priest is the pliers-type dispatcher that crushes the skull. Personally I find the priest swift, effective and humane.

Dog Welfare

If you are working a dog or dogs, whether as shooting companions, in the beating line or for picking up, their welfare is paramount. I always carry an old-fashioned shooting bag with an outside net to hold a spare whistle (and make sure it is the same pitch as your regular whistle), a first-aid kit for dogs, wire-cutters, a spare lead and my priest. You should always carry water for the dog(s) and today one can obtain plastic carriers, which double up as water holders and bowls. I don't put my Labradors into coats at the end of a day's work, but give them a hearty rub down with towelling. They are transported in a large cage adapted for a vehicle, which is lined with a warm section of rug. I also pack several mini-Mars Bars, allowing one to each dog at lunch time to help provide an energy boost.

At the end of the day check your dog for thorns, taking care to see that each pad is thorn and cut free; also make sure that it has not picked up any ticks.

A pair of wire-cutters can be a vital tool to carry, especially if your dog(s) is eager to jump fencing when picking up. On one shoot where I work my dogs there is a great deal of wire fencing carrying a single top strand, and on several occasions a dog has been trapped by a leg as it jumped because the top strand has twisted to hold the leg, leaving the animal hanging upside down. I have also seen more than one roe deer trapped in this fashion, suspended until it died – a horrible death. Barbed wire is another hazard, and all too often a dog will tear itself when racing out to a retrieve, or when returning carrying a bird, which may partly obscure its vision.

Useful Addresses

British Association for Shooting & Conservation (BASC)
Marford Mill, Rossett, Wrexham, Clwyd LL12 0HL
Tel: 01244 573000
www.basc.org.uk

BASC Scottish Office
Trochry, Dunkeld, Perthshire PH8 0DY
Tel: 01350 723226

British Shooting Sports Council
PO Box 53608, London SE24 9YN
Tel: 0207 0958181
www.bssc.org.uk

Countryside Alliance
367 Kennington Road, London SE11 4PT
Tel: 0207 8409200
www.countryside-alliance.org

Department for Environment Food and Rural Affairs (Defra)
European Wildlife Division, Temple Quay House, 2 The Square, Temple Way,
Bristol BS1 6EB
Tel: 117 3728746

The Game and Wildlife Conservation Trust
Fordingbridge, Hampshire SP6 1EF
Tel: 01425 652381
www.gwct.org.uk

Gun Trade Association and the Shooting Sports Trust
PO Box 43, Tewkesbury, Gloucestershire GL20 5ZE
Tel: 01684 291868
www.gtaltd.co.uk

The National Gamekeepers' Organisation (NGO)
PO Box 246, Darlington DL1 9FZ
Tel: 01833 660869
www.nationalgamekeepers.org.uk

National Organisation of Beaters and Pickers-up
The Cabin, 14 Kickdom Close, The Downs, Amesbury, Wilts SP4 7XB
Tel: 08456 345014
www.nobs.org.uk

Natural England
1 East Parade, Sheffield S1 2ET
Tel: 0114 2418920
www.naturalengland.org.ok

Scottish Association for Country Sports
Netherholm, Netherburn, Larkhall ML9 3DG
Tel: 01698 885206
www.sacs.org.uk

Scottish Gamekeepers' Association
Arran House, Arran Rd, Perth PH1 3DZ
Tel: 01738 587515
www.scottishgamekeepers.co.uk

Information on shooting in Europe
www.face-europe.org

Index